OPERATION
CONE OF POWER

By The Same Authors:

Philip Heselton:

Skyways and Landmarks Revisited
(with Jimmy Goddard and Paul Baines) (1985)
Earth Mysteries: An Exploratory Introduction
(with Brian Larkman) (1985)
Tony Wedd: New Age Pioneer (1986)
The Elements of Earth Mysteries (1991)
Secret Places of the Goddess (1995)
Earth Mysteries (1995)
Mirrors of Magic (1997)
Magical Guardians (1998)
Leylines: A Beginner's Guide (1999)
Wiccan Roots (2000)
Gerald Gardner and the Cauldron of Inspiration (2003)
Newland Avenue School 1896-2006 (2006)
Witchfather: A Life of Gerald Gardner (Vols. 1 and 2) (2012)
Doreen Valiente Witch (2016)
In Search of the New Forest Coven (2020)

Moira Hodgkinson:

The Witching Path (2007)
The Witch's Journey (2017)
The Folklore and Magic of Dolls (2019)
Wild Women (2017)
Blue Moon (2020)
Katy Hunter and the Magic Star (2020)
Living Witchcraft (2021)

OPERATION
CONE OF POWER

by

Philip Heselton

&

Moira Hodgkinson

Published by
Fenix Flames Publishing Ltd 2022

Copyright © 2022

Philip Heselton & Moira Hodgkinson

All rights reserved including the right of reproduction in whole or in part in any form. No reproduction, copy or transmission of this publication may be made without written permission. No paragraph of this publication may be reproduced, copied or transmitted save with written permission or in accordance with the provisions of the Copyright Act 1956 (as amended). Any person who performs any unauthorised act in relation to this publication may be liable to criminal prosecution and civil claims for damages. The moral rights of the author have been asserted.

Published by Fenix Flames Publishing Ltd

Design & Layout: Ashley Mortimer

Front Cover Illustration: Tim Stimson

Printed by Lightning Source International / Ingram Spark

Paperback ISBN 978-1-913768-13-3
Hardback ISBN 978-1-913768-15-7
eBook ISBN 978-1-913768-14-0

www.publishing.fenixflames.co.uk

In memory of all those who risked so much for others, and all those who continue to do so today.

We thank you.

Acknowledgements

With appreciation and thanks to Ian Stevenson, Hilary Byers and Tim Stimson and to our fellow members of the Triple Horse Coven who have given so much support to this project. Also to Ashley Mortimer and Angela Barker of Fenix Flames and Caz Galloway.

Contents

Cast of Characters

Act One - The Witches of the New Forest

The Shape of Things to Come 1
One - Gerald Joins the Witches' Circle 3
Two - An Announcement of War 9
Three - The Witch and Her Daughter 13
Four - At the Witch's House 19
Five - Gerald's Book 29
Six - Typescript and Marmalade 33
Seven - Ernie Opens Gerald's Eyes 37
Eight - No More Marmalade Tarts 45
Nine - A Witches' Circle 49
Ten - What Does Ernie Know? 53
Eleven - The Night Patrol 59
Twelve - A Book Arrives 65
Thirteen - 'A Grand Yarn' 71

Act Two - A Magical Call to Arms

Fourteen - Gerald's Fishing Finds a Loophole 77
Fifteen - Gerald Tells His Tale and The Masons Tell All .. 83
Sixteen - Tea and Tears 89
Seventeen - Keep Our Soldiers Safe! 95
Eighteen - Cream Tea 101
Nineteen - Scouting for Recruits 107
Twenty - Who and Where? 113
Twenty-One - Gerald Makes an Offer 119
Twenty-Two - Day Trippers 123
Twenty-Three - Edith Gets Busy 131
Twenty-Four - How to Influence Hitler 135
Twenty-Five - Raising the Power 141
Twenty-Six - Sending Forth 149

Act Three - Consequences

Twenty-Seven - Edith Solves Rosanne's Worries 155
Twenty-Eight - An Unexpected Sadness 159
Twenty-Nine - The Magna Carta Letter 163
Thirty - The Fire Dims at the Forge. 167
Thirty-One - Rosanne and Tommy Tie the Knot 169
Thirty-Two - Another Witch on Avenue Road. 173
Thirty-Three - 'Highcliffe Resident Annoys Nazis'. 177
Thirty-Four - But Did It Work?. 181
Thirty-Five - Farewell to Friends. 185

Afterwords 195
About the Authors 199

Cast of Characters
1939/1940

Gerald Brosseau Gardner Age 55. Born into an affluent timber-importing firm in Liverpool, he recently retired from a life "Out East" as a tea and rubber planter and civil servant. An amateur archaeologist and anthropologist, he now lives in Highcliffe.

Edith Rose Woodford-Grimes (neé Wray) (also known as Daff or Dafo) Age 51. Born in Yorkshire, she became a lady's maid. After the First World War, she taught adult education classes in Southampton. Separated from her husband, she lives in Somerford, near Christchurch, teaching elocution and speech therapy privately.

Susie Mary Mason Age 57. Lives in Southampton and works in the family business of lantern-slide manufacture.

Ernest William Mason (known as 'Ernie') Age 54. Susie's brother, lives in Southampton and works in the family business of lantern-slide manufacture.

Dorothea Frances ('Donna') Gardner Age 46. Gerald's wife. Currently working as a nurse in London.

Dorothy St. Quintin Fordham (neé Clutterbuck) Age 59. Wealthy widow, owning several large houses in Highcliffe.

Rosanne Woodford-Grimes Age 18. Edith's daughter.

Amelie Fribbens (Mrs.) Age 45. Gerald's housekeeper.

George Alexander Sullivan Age 49. Leader of the Rosicrucian Crotona Fellowship group in Somerford, near Christchurch.

Cecil Albert Thompson ('Tommy') Age 27. Rosanne's fiancé.

Major Frederick Merriott Fish Age 43. Commander of the Highcliffe Home Guard.

Katherine Louise Oldmeadow Age 62. Author of girls' school stories, herbalist.

Rosamund Isabella Charlotte Sabine (née Carnsew) Age 75. Experienced occultist and esotericist, herbalist.

Thomas George Alford Broadfield Sabine Age 67. Rosamund's husband.

Harry ('Dion') Byngham Age 44. Journalist, naturist and food reformer.

Walter John Forder Age 58. Journalist, Editor of the 'Christchurch Times'.

Charles Loader Age 76. Blacksmith and farrier for over 40 years.

ACT ONE

THE WITCHES OF THE NEW FOREST

The Shape of Things to Come

October 1940

There was a sense of loss hanging in the air, almost tangible, despite the success of what she had done. Was it, she asked herself yet again, the right thing to do? She had known full well that not everyone who had taken part was in good health and she had gone ahead regardless, bull-headed and determined to act.

If there had been time, younger people could have been encouraged to take part, people who were full of life and vitality. There were not many young people involved in this strange world of hers, however, and certainly none she knew well enough that she'd have felt comfortable asking them to be involved. None she trusted or could rely upon as surely as her close circle of friends and other acquaintances, who she knew to have the right attitude for the solemn occasion.

Now she had a death on her conscience. Indirectly, of course, but still, there was a measure of guilt that rested heavily on her shoulders and her sleep this last week had been restless and fitful. Perhaps she had acted too hastily in gathering her circle of friends together for the event, but with the threat of invasion looming ever closer, they had agreed to act swiftly. Unless, she thought, she had pressured them into it? She mused on this for a moment and shook her head. No, they had all agreed on the plan and volunteered to take part.

A gentle knock on the window disturbed her quiet reflection and self-chastisement and, looking up, she saw a familiar face peering in through the window.

"Come in." She stood up wearily and went to greet her visitor at the front door.

"Hello," she said, "What brings you here? Have a seat in the lounge and I shall make us some tea." She walked through the house towards the kitchen, followed by her guest. Turning, she was startled to see the expression on their face. Ashen white. Serious.

"What is it? Has something happened?" Suddenly her heart was pounding and she clutched her hands together with dread.

"I'm so sorry," the visitor said, their head shaking sadly from side to side. "What we did, it was too much for some us. Another member of our circle was taken ill a few days ago."

"My God, no!" The woman staggered slightly and guiding hands led her to the kitchen, gently pressing her to sit. "Is it serious?"

"I'm sorry, but he died last night."

"Who?" She raised a hand to her face, clammy and cold with fear. "Tell me who it is! Have I lost him? Is it him?"

~ ONE ~

Gerald Joins the Witches' Circle

Saturday 2nd September 1939

It was not the nudity that troubled him. After all, he had been a member of naturist clubs for several years and he was quite proud of his all-over suntan.

No, it was the vulnerability, standing alone in the dark with a blindfold over his eyes, not knowing what was going to happen or what he was about to be initiated into.

Gerald's mind went back almost thirty years to his time in Borneo, when he went through an initiation ritual in one of the traditional longhouses where he experienced a strange alteration of consciousness, and where he had obtained the dragon tattoos which now adorned his forearms. He didn't suppose that tattoos would play any part in the initiation he was about to go through, but still, there were any number of unknown elements involved.

Yet he trusted his friends - Susie and Ernie and Rosetta. Whilst he hadn't known them long, they had become as dear friends as any he had known. He knew that he would go through hell and high water for any of them.

And then there was Edith. He suspected that he was falling in love with Edith; he could talk to her about things he could never mention to his wife, Donna.

He heard footsteps outside the door, the creak of the hinges as it opened, and felt a hand on his shoulder. One word was issued, in a voice which he didn't recognise: "Come!"

He was led down what seemed to be a long, cold corridor. Then a door opened in front of him and the overpowering scent of incense immediately assailed him, pungent and smoky. He was helped down three steps by whoever was guiding him on, and he stood still for what seemed like minutes, and then, Edith's voice rang out unmistakeably, clearly, as befitted the amateur actress and teacher of elocution that he knew her to be.

"O thou who standest on the threshold ..."

***

Gerald hadn't been quite sure what to expect but it certainly wasn't this. Sheer euphoria, a sense of elation and joy at finally being a part of this group whom he had known for what seemed an eternity, but until now had always been slightly apart from. His hands shook with nervous energy and his heart beat loudly in his chest, matching almost completely the pulsating rhythm of the drummer's beat, dah-dum, dah-dum, dah-dum.

The excitement and tension in the room, built up to a dizzying crescendo as the dance came to its end, was tangible on his skin, with goose pimples on his arms. The ritual reached its climax and he was welcomed into the witch cult with hugs and cheers and kisses. Warm hands on his shoulders, gentle kisses on his cheeks and a rousing cheer. Bound to them all now, at last, in perfect love and perfect trust. He was part of something larger and more meaningful than merely a circle of friends and with every closely whispered word of congratulations, with every loud, proud cheer of 'hurrah', Gerald knew he would never be alone again. Never worry or fret or suffer alone. These were his chosen family now, these kind, warm and loving folk who had let him in on their most secret of secrets.

Now that the ceremony itself was over and light-hearted chatter began, he was able to take in his surroundings properly. He cast his gaze slowly across the paraphernalia of the craft. Imagination was a fine thing and Gerald's creative mind, combined with the exotic trinkets and sacred relics, carefully curated and brought home from his travels, had provided him with the most impressive visions of delicate silverware, statues and strange, magical objects. The venue itself was not quite as he had pictured it but nor was he disappointed. He appeared to be standing in the hall or drawing room of some old property, perhaps an old stone cottage. He had been brought here in secret, of course, the exact location unknown to him, but it was a pleasant space and duly decorated with suitably witchy accoutrements. It wasn't until later he realised that this was the home of Dorothy Fordham, who had kindly offered the use of it to the witches.

Two tall pillar candles, set atop heavy wrought iron stands, cast a speckled, flickering light on the statues of the horned god and the moon goddess, bringing their faces to life in the dance of shadows against the wall behind the altar. Black-handled knives, each one carefully carved or painted along the handle with sigils and symbols, lay on a velvet cloth and a silver chalice engraved with mystical sigils and rune marks was filled with deep red wine. His eyes skipped over the tools on the altar; scourge, sword, censer, bowls of water and salt, the cords. Presented to him as part of the ceremony, everything here had a magical purpose, each one revealed to him by a member of the group. The sword glinted in the candle light as Susie Mason picked it up. He watched her lay it reverently on the floor and wrap it in a long, black, silken cloth, pulling the fine fabric around the blade and its hilt with a reverence akin to love. A show of respect, not just of the coven sword, but of all it represented: unity, family, power and magic. A sword and a collection of black-handled knives - these were exactly the sort of tools that suited him most. He called to mind the collection of weaponry he owned himself, carefully collected during his long travels around the globe. Though many of the items in his possession were unique or valuable, not a single one of his pieces held nearly as much charm, mystery or power as these did, sitting as they did in a place of power, the witch's altar.

A muffled laugh came to his ears just as he was jostled from behind, his reverie broken.

"Sorry about that." Ernie Mason, an imposing character with dark hair turning to grey and eyes that were piercing behind the glass frames of his spectacles, clapped Gerald on the back and grabbed him by the arm, leaning in to whisper. "You'll soon get used to the odd naked bump here and there."

As a long-standing member of various naturist clubs over the years, that was not something he worried over, and he was about to say as much when Ernie was whisked off by Susie Mason. She had put on a robe but her hair was still loose about her shoulders, giving her a kind of beauty he had not noticed before. She picked up the broom and the cauldron from their places near the altar and held them out for Ernie to take. She nodded her head to the door and he went off to busy himself with the task of putting the things away, storing them safely for the next time.

"Was it everything you hoped it would be?" Susie asked him now. She rested one hand on her hip and linked the other into Gerald's arm, squeezing him gently.

Gerald nodded slowly. "All of that and more."

That seemed to satisfy her for she grinned and patted his arm lightly, gave him a quick kiss on each cheek and took off on the tips of her toes, humming to herself and skipping lightly as she made her way out of the room.

Gerald glanced around the circle as the small group set about putting the room back in order, tidying away a drop of spilled candle wax and wrapping the assorted collection of black-handled knives in a protective black cloth. Dark robes were thrown over bare shoulders and one by one, the participants gradually drifted away from the hijacked drawing room and he was alone with her.

The Witch.

"Congratulations." The woman approached him, placing her hands on his shoulders.

She was a handsome woman, this witch, with wide brown eyes that were full of knowledge, cunning and an allure he could not name. If he stared into them long enough, those beguiling eyes would drink in all of his hidden thoughts and deepest secrets while all the time not letting anything out that she didn't want known. Her heart-shaped face, made up with pristine precision, was soft and kind, her skin flawless, full lips the colour of a rose.

Gerald swayed slightly, the electric energy of the initiation ceremony still affecting him. Was it like this for everyone? The full and heady scent of the incense that still hung thick in the air, the odd sensation of being moved about the circle by hands he couldn't see through the blind-fold that had covered his eyes, the warmth of his fellow coveners around him, voices speaking to him that he hadn't recognised: it had all added to the power and built up the mystery. Disorientation. Was that all it was? No, the sensations that pricked his skin like teasels were esoteric, ethereal in nature and unlike anything he had ever experienced before now.

"Are you feeling quite all right?" An expression of mild concern crossed her face.

True beauty and majesty lay within her soul, he could see it shining in her eyes and feel it piercing his heart, like an arrow meeting its mark. Gerald breathed in deeply, catching a remaining hint of the sharp smelling incense in his nostrils. The scent of ritual, magic and witchcraft. A scent that would forever remind him of this night, this ceremony of initiation and belonging that he had been inexorably heading toward all his life.

"I think I can say in all honestly that I have never felt better than I do right now."

"Then welcome, brother witch."

She pulled herself into his arms and for a long moment they stood firm and close, skin to skin and soul to soul, and when they parted, they did so with a kiss. The odd, woozy sensation he'd been feeling was replaced by one of solidness, normality restored.

She had grounded him instantly, with a single, chaste kiss. What power and magnificence she must hold that she could do such a thing so readily? Ah, Edith! His heart raced, alive with all the fire and charm and magic of the witch's circle.

They danced, the witch and the man, until long into the night.

~ TWO ~

An Announcement of War

Sunday 3rd September 1939

Three hours, a little more, perhaps. That was all the slumber he could manage after the experiences, so wild and joyful, of the night before and instead of tossing and turning, he had risen early to fix his morning cup of tea, plenty of sugar and just the right amount of milk, thank you very much, and a plate of hot buttered toast spread thickly with marmalade. In spite of the lack of sleep that caused a deep tiredness in the marrow of his bones, he simply couldn't set his mind to rest, no matter how quiet and peaceful the environment. The fibres of his being were restless, arms and legs twitching with a fidgeting of nerves, his sharp mind alive with darting thoughts and the need to capture them, every single one, so that in years to come he could read and relive every single, precious moment of that most magical time.

> *I knew then that that which I had thought burnt out hundreds of years ago still survived.*

His pen flew across the blank pages of his journal, filling out page after page of the book with the scrambled, disjointed and hurried thoughts that threatened to overwhelm his very soul if he didn't write them down and record in as much detail as he could every moment of the magnificent event. Initiation. The very word itself held associations that stretched back through the years, decades, centuries, connecting him to the countless witches who had come before him, across the country, across the world. Initiation, the start of a journey into the unknown, a symbolic death and rebirth into a new life.

Of course, this was not the first time Gerald had ventured into the realms of magical practices, though those which he had learned of and experienced in Malaya and elsewhere had been quite different to this. Still, the tantalising possibilities of this home-grown witchcraft were vast and compelling, and Gerald swore that he would chase up every new experience, follow every lead into the esoteric and exotic that came upon him. Not only was this the marker of a turning point in his life but a moment of passing through a gateway that would lead into unknown worlds awaiting discovery and exploration.

How best to describe it?

> *It was the most wonderful night of my life. In true witch fashion we had a dance afterwards, and kept it up until dawn.*

And then, distracted by the sudden grave tones of the wireless, which was playing half-forgotten in the background, Gerald slowly put down his pen and sat up straight, his back aching. He returned his attention to the broadcast.

> *This morning the British ambassador in Berlin handed the German government a final note stating that unless we heard from them by 11 o'clock that they were prepared at once to withdraw their troops from Poland, a state of war would exist between us. I have to tell you now that no such undertaking has been received, and that consequently this country is at war with Germany.*

The terrible news that he had pushed to one side during the preparation for his initiation, had not been unexpected, he mused, but still it was a grim pronouncement and he didn't envy the Prime Minister's position one jot. Who would want such a great political career at a time when it seemed half the world was on the verge of war with one country or another? It had been a growing concern for what seemed an eternity but now that it was here... In the space of a heart-beat the world as he knew it had changed. Gerald listened intently as the Prime Minister's voice filled his book-lined library with grave words to update the public. The excitement of his recent initiation into a cult he had once thought no longer in existence had taken so great a hold of him that he felt elated. But there was no pushing it aside or denying the stark reality any longer, the radio broadcast brought it to the forefront, and he hung his head sadly.

Britain was at war with Germany.

~ THREE ~

The Witch and Her Daughter

Tuesday 5th September 1939

Daybreak, gentle and unassuming, crept into the room with hazy light and beyond the window a host of birds chirruped and sang without a care. "Liars," Edith chided them, "liars all with their songs of ruddy cheerfulness". For despite the long days and nights of late summer and the bright, happy sound of the birds calling to each other as the day began anew, there was nothing to be cheerful about today. She could barely stand to think of it, let alone rise up and face the day to deal with the stark reality of it all. Preparations for the ceremony had taken up most of her time, and indeed, her thoughts for the past few weeks. Looming political tensions had gripped the nation while she'd had her mind so full of magical mysteries that it was only now the stark reality of the situation hit her.

It seemed incredible that the threat of one small word could so dramatically change the world she lived in, yet there it was. Tensions had been rising across Europe for longer than she wanted to remember and now the unthinkable had happened. Germany had invaded Poland and that solitary word was no longer a far-off threat but a worrying reality. War.

Her head was heavy on the pillow and she let it lie there a moment longer, clinging to the warmth and false comfort of pleasant dreams before sighing loudly and resigning herself to the dreariness of morning routines. Edith rose out of bed, shrugging off her gloomy thoughts. She'd never been a woman who lazed about in bed in the morning and she certainly didn't intend to get into the habit now, even though her day would most likely be interspersed with an uneasy sense of dread and uncertainty. Action, though, the familiar routines of work and home, would soon bring her out of the slump and if not, well, there were plenty of other things she could do to rouse her spirits.

Slippers on her feet, house-coat tied neatly about the waist, Edith glanced at her reflection in the mirror standing on the dresser in front of her bedroom window. Her dark hair, which was gently waved rather than being either curly or straight, was a dreadful sight, and underneath her eyes were the tell-tale dark shadows of having had too little sleep. Still, she smiled as she set about fixing her hair with pins to give it some semblance of respectability, the late hour a few nights ago had been worth it, even if she hadn't caught up on her precious sleep yet. Sighing at her reflection, Edith resigned herself to a complete stand-still of her social life for the foreseeable future, so she was glad to have done something exciting to tide her over as the grim news started to take hold of the nation. She pinched her cheeks lightly to give them some colour and then put her hand out for the doorknob when she was startled half out of her wits by a loud knocking on the door. A small squeak of surprise escaped her mouth.

"Mother, aren't you dressed yet?" Rosanne flung the door wide and burst inside.

"Rosanne," she countered, "there's no need to pound like an ape. A single knock is enough."

"I've just read yesterday's paper again. Did you see the proposals for food rations? Rationing? Surely it won't come to that." Rosanne carried on in a garbled rush of disjointed words and she paced the hallway. Up and down, up and down, footsteps ringing out sharply in the early morning quietness of the bungalow. Edith stopped her with a firm hand on her shoulder and guided her along the hall.

"Stop it, please. You're making me dizzy." She stepped into the kitchen and busied herself with breakfast things, filling the kettle with water and setting out her favourite willow pattern china cups and saucers. "Sugar, dear?"

Rosanne nodded politely, but she didn't look up, Edith noticed, her head was bowed low and worry wrinkled her brow. She let the girl sit for a moment to gather her thoughts while she set about placing the cups and saucers, sugar bowl, tongs and milk on the table. Breakfast on a weekday morning was a simple affair of hot buttered toast with a good-sized dollop of blackberry and apple jam spread on top, home-made, of course. The warm season had brought plenty of ripe berries already and despite the inevitable prickles and scratches from the thorny bramble bushes, Edith couldn't help but spend a few hours roaming the wild areas near her home picking the fruit. It was one of the many things she enjoyed doing to bring a little of the natural, wholesome world into her home. She sucked a smear of creamy butter from her fingertips and eyed the clock over the fireplace.

She would have to dress properly for the day the minute breakfast was done with. The morning was wasting away already, but first there was a sobbing young woman to contend with. The emotions of youth ran high and giddily and this wasn't the first time she'd found herself caught up in the dramas and traumas of Rosanne's hot temper and mood swings. The girl was starting to calm down as the years passed and it wouldn't be long now before she became the strong, confident woman she was destined to be.

Rosanne sniffed and lifted a hand to her face, brushing moisture from her eyes. "I was supposed to be meeting Alice at the cinema last night but the Regent's closed. Well, actually, she had to cry off after spraining her ankle, but that's not the point. And it's not just the cinema either, all public gatherings are cancelled until further notice; concerts, theatres, and they have even banned football matches for goodness' sake! It's all so sudden and I - I can't bear it, Mother. What's next? Will we have no buses or trains?"

"Oh Rosanne, darling," Edith spoke softly and hoped her voice was reassuring. "I'm sorry that you missed your film, but these restrictions won't last forever."

"You don't know that." Rosanne huffed with deliberate, unnecessary volume, and folded her hands across her chest, unfolded them again and then picked up a spoon, which she proceeded to play with restlessly. "Nobody does. Nobody knows anything. Chamberlain's latest speech. You heard it, I assume?"

"Everyone has. I think it was inevitable that it would come to this, really. But there's no need to panic, we're not about to be blown up in our homes."

"Not yet." Rosanne's cup shook as she put down the spoon and sipped her tea and she put the cup clumsily onto the saucer. "But we've all been asked to play our part and I know what that means. It means our men will be sent off to be shot at or blown up and killed while we women stay behind with nothing to do but dig vegetables while we worry and grieve and wait for them to start coming back to us in pieces."

"But Rosanne," Edith was about to say something reassuring but her daughter interrupted her, a horrified look on her face.

"What about your friend, Mr Gardner? You've become quite close, haven't you?" She didn't give time for Edith to reply. "Will he be required to enlist do you think?"

'Surely not," Edith patted her hand lightly and said to Rosanne the same thing she had herself when the thought had crossed her own mind. "Gerald is too long in the tooth for it, though he was talking about becoming an Air Raid Warden. I think that should be quite enough for him."

"What about the other men we know, the younger ones? What about Tommy? It's too much!"

Rosanne wailed again and Edith's heart ached, for there was nothing she could do or say to make it right. No comforting words she could offer, no protective haven to run to where they would be kept safe. Yet she was a mother and so she would do her best. Edith had been the embodiment of the word composed for most of her life and that's exactly what she must be now, for the sake of her daughter, only eighteen, who depended on her so heavily.

"Rosanne, would you please wait and see what happens before you go blowing hot and cold? It could all be over in a matter of months. Hitler will come to his senses, you'll soon see."

Rosanne's face was lined with unhappiness, far from convinced or reassured, but there was nothing more to say that would give that much needed reassurance, and waves of despair and helplessness flowed between them. It was no good; try as she might to find it, that composure was out of reach, banished by that one word that hung over them both, over the country, over the world for all she knew, like a black cloud of violent rain. Grasped by the cold fingers of dread, Edith knew she would succumb to fear and worry if she didn't take control of herself so she determined here and now that she wouldn't let that happen.

Beneath the table, she uncrossed her legs, slipped off her slippers and placed the soles of both feet firmly on the ground. The wooden floor beneath her toes was unyielding and solid, a source of firm grounding, and with slow, deliberate breaths, she pulled strength and power from the deep core of the earth, up her meridians and into her soul, where she visualised it swirling in a glow of bright hope, mixing in with the energy of her chakras to boost her inner strength. It took only a few deep, long breaths, each one accompanied by thoughts of white light, to bring a little cheer and solace back into her mind.

"Come on now, pull yourself together." Edith handed a clean handkerchief to Rosanne who took it gratefully and pressed it to her face. "Wipe your eyes and splash some cold water on your face before you head out. I'm sure you don't want to arrive at work looking red-faced and flushed like that."

Her own composure was back in full force and thank the heavens for a full day of work ahead of her because without that to focus on, she might very well lose herself in the seriousness of it once Rosanne was out of sight.

~ FOUR ~

At The Witch's House

Thursday 7th September 1939

Gerald was, he admitted to himself, feeling apprehensive. He had got to know Edith quite well by the time of his initiation, but this was the first time he had been invited to her home. He had put on a decent shirt and a pair of long trousers instead of the customary shorter ones he preferred, as he knew Edith would probably expect him to look smart.

It didn't take him long to cycle the few miles to Somerford. He had her address memorised - No. 16 Dennistoun Avenue - and his heart missed a beat, or beat faster, he wasn't quite sure, as he saw the name sign on the corner of the newly-built street of modest bungalows.

A little way up, he dismounted and wheeled his bicycle along the pavement, looking at the house numbers as he did so. He counted, "10, ... 12, ..." He was surprisingly nervous as he approached Edith's house. He didn't know what he was expecting, but there were butterflies in his tummy, which he knew was his over-active solar plexus. From poring over his many books on the esoteric and from his own experience, he knew that butterflies in that area, often acted almost as a psychic medium. He was normally a very confident man, not one to let his nerves get the better of him but these sensations in his tummy of nervous anticipation were undeniable and, in a way, quite exciting. Was it because he was visiting her on "home ground" as it were, or was it something more?

There was no time for further introspection because here he was, outside no. 16. The house number, if there had ever been one, had been replaced by a name sign, which read "Theano". Gerald puzzled over the unusual name briefly, trying to recall where he knew it from and then he made the connection to the play he had watched recently at the Rosicrucian Theatre. It was based on the life of the Greek philosopher, Pythagoras, whose wife was Theano. She had been played by Edith and, although Edith had been a member of the naturist club he had joined, her performance in the play was the first time he had really noticed her. She had been a much better actor than any of the other performers.

Gerald opened the gate and wheeled his bicycle into the side drive. Leaning it carefully against the bungalow wall, he approached the door, which was a little further down the drive.

Beside the door was a carefully polished brass plaque, reading:

> "E. Woodford Grimes
> ALCM, ALAM (Eloc.)
> Teacher of Elocution
> and Dramatic Art"

He rang the bell and almost immediately a young woman, whom he judged to be in her late teens, opened the door. Gerald was so overwhelmed by her beauty that, to start with, he couldn't say anything. Slim and well-dressed, looking much like her mother, she smiled at him warmly and stuck out her hand.

"You must be Mr. Gardner. Do come in."

He shook hands with the young woman and managed to restrain himself from his usual riposte of, "it's Dr. Gardner, actually", and merely said, "and you must be Rosanne. Your mother has told me a lot about you."

She smiled at him, holding the door open and inviting him in. "Not too much, I hope. Come into the sitting room. I think mother is just in the kitchen preparing something or other. Have a seat, Mr. Gardner, and I shall tell her you've arrived."

Gerald looked around him. The room was dominated by a rather old-fashioned suite of well-upholstered pale green furniture. On the small coffee table lay a copy of today's newspaper, pages left open at a piece describing the latest happenings from parliament. The Telegraph, he noted, with approval. He glanced briefly at the article before turning his attention to the most interesting things in the room. The alcoves had built-in bookshelves, each one full from floor to ceiling. He had always loved books, from the days in Madeira when he had taught himself to read, and he had accumulated a large collection of his own over the years.

The first thing he noticed was how neat and tidy they were: all the books were standing upright and arranged by both height and subject-matter. He contrasted this with his own collection, which, whilst considerably larger than Edith's, was haphazard and in no discernible order. How lovely it must be to reach for a particular volume and know exactly where it would be. His own deeper shelves had two rows of books, one behind the other, and he could never remember where a particular book was to be found, especially if it was on the inner, hidden row. Many of his books were stacked horizontally, not just on the shelves but piled up in every corner of the room that he described as his "library". He could imagine Edith's eyes rolling up in despair at the chaos of his collection.

Several sets of encyclopaedias were immediately evident by their fine binding. Dictionaries in English and other languages, and much classic English literature and poetry. He spotted one volume entitled 'Modern Russian Poetry' and marvelled at the breadth of her knowledge and interests.

All of this Gerald expected, but there were also Greek and Latin texts, mighty tomes of history from ancient times to the present day and, what seized his interest most; a considerable number of volumes of what he would classify as occult or esoteric. He recognised quite a few that he had in his own library, but his eye was attracted by one volume entitled 'The Witch Cult in Western Europe'.

"That's how the witches I've met refer to themselves. I didn't know there was a book about it!" He whispered, as if not wanting to disturb the books. He took the book off the shelf and was about to start perusing it, when Edith entered the room.

"Ah! I thought the books might keep you occupied. But, before we discuss the book you have in your hands, you must answer an important question."

"Of course! Ask away, Edith."

"Do you prefer tea or coffee? I have both."

A smile spread across Gerald's face. "Well, I suppose I got used to drinking tea during the time I spent as a tea-planter in Ceylon. They used to grow coffee there, but there was a terrible disease affecting the coffee crop called 'Devastating Emily'. By the time I was there, you couldn't really get coffee, so tea it was. I think I've told you about my old nursemaid, Com, and her husband, David? He was the tea planter I worked for. They live in Bournemouth now. I'd like you to meet them, I think you would like Com very much."

"Yes, I would be pleased to meet them. So, the answer to my question is tea?"

"Yes, please, Dafo!"

Edith made no answer as she left the room. She didn't know why he had taken to calling her 'Dafo'. Her family had been using the nickname 'Daff' for as long as she could remember, but she hadn't known Gerald for long and part of her thought it was rather presumptuous of him, the other part of her thought it was rather nice.

As soon as she was out of the room, Gerald picked up the book he had been looking at, 'The Witch Cult in Western Europe'. It was by one Margaret Alice Murray and was subtitled 'A Study in Anthropology'. As he was now a witch and also considered himself an anthropologist, he thought it would be the sort of thing he should read. He leafed through a few pages which seemed to be about the witch trials of hundreds of years ago and, glancing at the chapter headings, he saw that it was about the witches' god, details of their rites, initiation ceremonies, organisation and gatherings, and much else besides.

He was just noting down the details of the book, intending to order a copy, when Edith returned with a large ornate tray on which she had placed an equally elegant teapot, teacups, milk jug, and a plate of delicious-looking marmalade tarts.

"I see Dr. Murray's book on the witch cult has attracted your interest. It is one of the very few books available on our history. It is interesting to see how some aspects of the cult have changed over the years, whereas others have stayed exactly the same. You can borrow it if you like."

"Thank you very much, Edith. I think I need to read up on something I've recently been initiated into. However," he continued, "there is something important I have to ask you. Please may I have one of those delicious-looking marmalade tarts?"

"Of course, Gerald, I baked them especially for your visit. But I hope you realise what an honour it is to have one, especially as they may be the last for a while, I fear. We're running very low on marmalade and it's virtually impossible to get the right sort of oranges at the moment and jars of marmalade in the shops are ridiculously expensive." She watched in amusement, as Gerald brushed crumbs from his moustache and immediately picked up another tart.

"I suppose it's the result of the war," Edith continued, "supplies are already being compromised. The government will introduce rationing before much longer, you mark my words. You had better enjoy your tarts while you can, Gerald."

At this, he helped himself to his third tart, eating it just as quickly as the first two he had consumed while Edith had been talking.

Edith sat down on the settee opposite Gerald. He was about to take his fourth marmalade tart when the look on her face told him that this was not really the time.

"Now, Gerald, we trusted you enough to initiate you…"

"And I trusted you all to allow you to initiate me," he interrupted her, "even though I didn't really know what it was that I was being initiated into. I just knew by then that I loved and trusted you all and you wouldn't do anything to harm me."

"Well, that is indeed gratifying, Gerald. But, to continue what I was saying, we haven't really had a chance to get to know each other properly, despite the feelings of familiarity we have with each other."

"Well, as soon as I met you, and the Masons, I felt I had known you before, a long time ago. You mentioned reincarnation?"

"Yes." Edith nodded, a serious expression on her face. "As I told you before your initiation, I am convinced you were known to some of us witches in a previous life and that is why we have been drawn together now. We can discuss that another time, perhaps. Do tell me more about your life. I know you worked out East, at least for a time."

Gerald relaxed in his chair, knowing that Edith wanted him to talk about one of his favourite subjects - himself.

He ventured to take yet another marmalade tart and started to speak: "I was there for thirty-six years altogether. It was rather an accident really. It all happened because I had asthma as a child. It was quite a serious condition and I might have died. Many did. Because of it, I couldn't go to school like my brothers. My parents were advised that the only … I won't say 'cure' but amelioration … would be for me to live most of the year in a warmer climate, and I should have pointed out that they were reasonably well-off and could afford it, they sent me abroad every winter with my nurse-maid. On one occasion we went to Nice, in the south of France, but most years we stayed in Madeira for several months at a time.

I think the idea was that Com ... my nursemaid, as I said, Georgina McCombie, though everyone else called her Jo ... well, she would be a sort of governess and teach me things." Here, Gerald paused in his reverie to stroke a few stray crumbs of pastry from the ends of his neatly trimmed moustache before continuing. "What actually happened is that she left me more or less on my own to explore and learn things in a rather haphazard way. I had to teach myself how to read, for example."

Edith butted in at this point, partly to hear another voice in the room apart from his. "That explains a few things."

"What things?"

"Never mind. We'll talk about that later."

"Anyway, Com got married to David Elkington, who was a tea planter in Ceylon. I was sixteen then, and my parents and David between them decided that I should be an apprentice tea planter on David's estate in Ceylon. I would, of course, also remain in touch with Com. So that is what I did."

"What about the asthma?" Edith inquired.

"Well, the doctors were right in that it did not recur during the whole of my time Out East. I was rather apprehensive when I retired three years ago that it would come back when I came to live in the smoky and polluted atmosphere of London, but it hasn't, so far."

"Let's hope so. Anyway, tell me a bit more about your time 'Out East'. It obviously made a deep impression on you."

"Well, yes. I was never one for socialising with most of the Europeans." Gerald waved his hand in the air, dismissively. "They bored me with their incessant small talk and customs, such as dressing for dinner. I didn't have much time for the pomp and bother of formal dress, you see. I used to take every opportunity to get to know the native people of Ceylon. I got to know them as friends, learned their languages as much as I could and, eventually, when they trusted me enough, they invited me into their homes and, ultimately, to their rituals."

"How exciting!"

"Oh, it was! I was happy wherever I was Out East, in Ceylon, Borneo or Johore."

"But you came back to England when you retired?"

"That was really my wife's doing, Donna. She never really settled in Johore, so, when I came to retirement age, she was very persistent in pushing me to come back to here. We came back in 1936, or at least Donna came back. It took me a few months to settle matters, primarily organising the publication of my book on the magical 'kris'."

"Yes, you very kindly gave me a copy."

"What did you make of it? I had hoped to interest the archaeologists and anthropologists with it, but it was not to be."

"I have an idea why that might be. But tell me about your wife. I think I've only seen her once, and that was at our performance of Pythagoras. Do tell me about her. I would at least like to meet her long enough to have a chat."

"I'm sure that can be arranged, but she is away at the moment. She was a nursing sister at St. Thomas's. I met her, fell in love with her, and married her, on my visit to England in 1927."

"That was rather hasty, Gerald!"

Gerald had expected such surprise from Edith; he had surprised a number of people at the time, with his wedding to Donna so soon after they had met. "I suppose you could call it a 'whirlwind romance'. Anyway, she's been called up, as she was on the reserve of nurses. She's a Certified Nursing Assistant, whatever that means exactly! She is currently lodging with friends in Epsom. She may well be back at St. Thomas's, but she never really tells me what she's doing. But there's bound to be a great need for nurses, particularly if the threat of air raids becomes a reality."

"You must be proud of her. But, if you don't mind my saying so, it seems that you and your wife are a little distant."

"Not at all, Dafo." He told her. "Donna and I simply have diverse interests and we each pursue them as we wish. It works very well for us."

There was a silence then, as Gerald found himself wondering about the nature of relationships, and he reached for the tea-pot. Edith chided him mildly, insisting on pouring the tea herself for her guest.

"Oh, I must tell you," Gerald took his tea and added two sugar cubes, "that I've been accepted as an Air Raid Warden, if I'm needed. I suppose the coastal areas are more likely to be affected, after all."

"A fine way of putting your spare time to good use, although I know you are still working on your book. Have you got a title for it yet?"

"I thought perhaps 'The Goddess Comes Forth' or 'Aphrodite Appears' or something like that. There's plenty of time to decide that. But did you like it?"

"It certainly has promise, Gerald, insofar as I could read it. Your handwriting is terrible!"

"I know, sometimes I can't read it myself, but the thoughts come to me so rapidly that I couldn't keep up if I wrote it legibly."

"While we're on the subject, your spelling is atrocious too. I imagine this is all as a result of having had to teach yourself to read."

"You are right there, and I do know I could use a little help. I rather hoped you would help me, Dafo."

"You need more than help. The manuscript needs a complete re-write. But I refuse to look at any more of your handwriting. Haven't you got access to a typewriter?"

"I did have one when I was in Johore, but I had to leave it behind. It was a big and heavy one."

"You should be able to get a lighter, portable one locally. See what you can find. If necessary, you can use mine and come around here when you want to use it."

"Oh, thank you, Daff. I'm sure that would be the best arrangement."

"But don't expect any more marmalade tarts, though."

"Not even if I promise to bring the marmalade?" He asked, hoping to win her over with his charm.

"Well, I'll consider it." Edith smiled at his eagerness for sweet treats.

"Anyway," said Gerald, "I've been working on the book since my initiation and I've made the heroine of the story, Dayonis, into a witch, and she casts a circle in which to make magic."

"I hope you haven't given away any secrets of the Craft." She gave him a stern look and Gerald nodded, suitably concerned.

"I don't think so, but that's partly why I'd like you to look over it," he said.

"I'll do that, Gerald, but I suspect I'm going to have to give it a major re-write, which I am quite prepared to do."

"That's exactly what Betty Lumsden Milne said when I presented her with the manuscript of the keris book."

"I can sympathise with her," Edith chuckled. "Well, look, Gerald, come over on Thursday and we'll go through it together and I may be able to make a few helpful suggestions."

~ FIVE ~

Gerald's Book

Tuesday 14th September 1939

After leaving her coat and hat with Mrs Fribbens and accepting the offer of a cup of tea, Edith climbed upstairs to the library. She could not resist looking at the display of armoury upon the walls: pistols, swords and fancy hilted daggers. She had a suspicion that most of the guns were not only in full working order but were regularly maintained, oiled and polished. There were several Malay keris, short knives or daggers, the shining blades shaped like a flicker of flame and the hilt of each bearing a different type of carved animal. As for the suit of armour on the landing, well, she was pleased she wasn't responsible for dusting that! What must poor Mrs Fribbens think of the household she looked after? Still, Edith supposed the housekeeper had grown used to his eccentric ways and his growing collection by now, and from what she had gathered, Gerald was a very easy and generous person to work for.

Gerald's library had three large desks, two of them barely visible beneath the wide range of books spread upon them, while seated at the remaining desk was the man himself. One hand propped up his chin and the other held a pen, poised over a of stack of ten sheets or so of plain paper, his scrawling writing all over the top page.

Deep in concentration, he had not noticed that she had come inside the room and now stood at the desk in front of him.

"Is that your manuscript?" Edith asked him, tapping a finger on the paper. Startled, Gerald jolted, shaking the hand that held his pen. Another scrawl was added to the lines of text. "I thought the version I looked at was complete."

"Good grief! How long have you been standing there?"

"Only a moment. Well, is it? Let me see."

Gerald took the sheaf of papers and squirreled them into a drawer of the desk. "No, this is my memoirs. The book is finished, as you say, and I shall always be grateful that you agreed to cast your careful eye over it."

"Indeed, I am very glad you did ask me for, although the story is very good, the same cannot be said for your writing."

"Whatever do you mean?" He blinked up at her with a look of astonishment on his face.

Edith came around the desk to sit beside him and insisted on looking at another page or two before she said anything more.

"You have a way with words, it's true," she began, "and your life has been so rich and curious that you are good at drawing the reader in, but we agreed that your grammar and spelling constantly falls short of expectations. The last time we spoke of your book, you were pondering over a title, as I recall. Have you made a decision yet?"

"I thought perhaps 'Aphrodite Rises'."

"The general public readership will hardly be aware of who She is, unless they have some knowledge of classical mythology. Perhaps simply 'The Goddess Rises'."

Gerald hummed to himself thoughtfully. "I will consider it, I found that your ideas are normally good ones. Now, what really brings you here this afternoon?"

"I was on my way to visit a friend nearby and wanted to ask you something while I am in the vicinity. Specifically, I want to know what you think of that young fellow Rosanne is courting. You're a good judge of character and you've met him on several occasions now."

Gerald nodded slowly. "Is he good enough for your daughter? I doubt anyone would be. However, Tommy does seem a likeable chap. I'm surprised you're seeking my opinion; it won't matter a jot to Rosanne if I approve of him or not, surely?"

Edith smiled and shook her head briefly. She rested a hand on top of the desk and sighed. "If you were not aware of it before now, I should tell you that you've made a very favourable impression on the girl - and on her mother."

Gerald put one of his large, warm hands over hers and returned her gaze.

"And I have become very fond of her - and of her mother."

With a rising heat flushing through her cheeks, Edith became intensely aware of their close proximity, so close she could almost feel the whisper of his warm breath on her face. Almost. She sat upright quickly and rose from the chair before she lost control of herself. Gerald was a married man and no matter how much she might wish otherwise, Edith would just have to keep that in mind.

~ SIX ~

Typescript and Marmalade

Thursday 21st September 1939

Edith had been wondering what approach she should take in going through his manuscript with Gerald. The spelling and grammar were the least of her problems. Any word which she just couldn't make head or tail of, she read out phonetically in her head and the word which Gerald meant would usually come to mind. As a last resort, she could always ask Gerald himself for clarification.

No, what really bothered her was that he was sailing much too close to the wind in letting Craft secrets out. He'd need to be watched. He had included a whole ritual that she hadn't been happy with, and he'd included animal sacrifice in a most unsavoury way. Her first instinct was to cut that section out completely, but she thought, 'No! Keep it in. It is just a work of fiction, after all, and this was supposed to have happened in Cyprus several thousand years ago.'

A little before the appointed time, Gerald was at the door, bearing what looked like a batch of typescript and four jars of marmalade.

"Come in, Gerald. Wherever did you get those jars of marmalade?"

"I had to cycle into Bournemouth, but I managed, by various means that I won't go into, to acquire these. Are they acceptable as a passport for entry?"

"They certainly are!" Edith was delighted, both with the marmalade and the fact that he had clearly gone to some considerable lengths to get it for her. "I'll put them in the kitchen. But what is this pile of paper you have with you?"

"Well, I took your advice and was able to borrow a typewriter from Mrs. Newby Stubbs, Luther's wife. I gave her a copy of my 'keris' book in exchange. You probably know him. He's performed in some of the plays at the theatre."

"Yes, his name sounds familiar, though I've never got to know him well."

"He's a nice chap. Anyway, I've done what you wanted me to do and typed it out.

"You have certainly been busy. It was only a week ago that we talked about it."

"Well, apart from my duties as an Air Raid Warden, I haven't got much else to do, so I thought I might as well get on with it."

"Good, give me a few days to review the material thoroughly. You won't object to listening to the news, I assume?"

"Good grief, is it that time already?" Gerald checked his watch and nodded. "Let's hear it, then."

Listening to the radio broadcast left Edith feeling distraught and helpless. Trouble had escalated to horrifying levels in Poland over the last few weeks, and overnight in particular, with an exchange of fire on the Polish-German border post at Jeziorki. The Germans had breached the border, the invasion under way.

Prime Minister Neville Chamberlain appeared before the House of Commons shortly after 6:00 in the evening.

> *"It now only remains for us to set our teeth and to enter upon this struggle, which we ourselves earnestly endeavoured to avoid, with determination to see it through to the end. We shall enter it with a clear conscience, with the support of the Dominions and the British Empire, and the moral approval of the greater part of the world."*

After several more minutes of depressing, frightening talk of bombs and explosions, the newsreader moved on to other topics and Edith switched off the wireless. She clenched her hands together to stop them trembling.

Noticing her unease, Gerald ventured to pat her on the hand and offered a small smile. "We're all right just here, aren't we? On a different subject, Dafo, I wonder if we could talk about our esoteric activities? I have one or two questions I should like the answers to, if you wouldn't mind."

She pulled herself together and dragged her thoughts back to the present moment and Gerald's keen curiosity. "Of course, what is it you'd like to know?"

Gerald spent the next ten minutes regaling Edith with his thoughts on his initiation ritual and how it had brought to him a sense of belonging and family. Their conversation carried on for some time before Edith finally stood up and attempted to steer him out of the house. As much as she was enjoying his company, the evening had grown late, and her body cried out for sleep.

"Well, this has been lovely, and I have enjoyed our conversation, Gerald. We have covered everything from setting up the altar and the meaning of its working tools to sensing the magical energy of the circle."

"There was one more thing, if you can spare another minute? I'm curious about the aura and how…"

"Gerald, stop. You're like a bulldog with a rag it won't let go of. If you really want to talk to someone over the next few days, I suggest you take up some of Ernie's time instead of mine." And with that, Edith said farewell and shooed him out of the door before he could delay her any more with talk of magic and mystery.

~ SEVEN ~

Ernie Opens Gerald's Eyes

Saturday 23rd September 1939

"An enquiring mind," Ernie told him, "sharp wits and a desire to expand that mind, my friend."

It occurred to Gerald, as he watched his friend walk from one side of the room to the other and back again while they talked, that a pipe would suit Ernie far better than the stubby, chewed up pencil that strayed from his hands to sit between his teeth. A bad habit, though, a pipe, and it was a good thing that his HB pencil took its place in Ernie's life, for the smoke of a pipe would be no good at all for the books. Dozens upon dozens of them spilled out from the bookshelves, double-stacked, to sit on every conceivable surface of the library-come-study where they had taken to having their little chats. Ernie's home in Osborne Road, where he lived with his sister, Susie, was situated in the Portswood area of Southampton and, conveniently for Gerald, was within easy walking distance of the St Denys' railway station.

Beechwood was a late Victorian house, very private and with extensive grounds and a substantial wooded garden. Several large beech trees provided patches of dappled shade in summer. And in the grounds Ernie kept an observatory which he had built himself, and which he was, quite rightly, very proud of.

They were currently in a room whose original purpose was perhaps a drawing room but could now be best described as a library. The collection of books, some of which he borrowed from time to time, was not the only reason Gerald enjoyed visiting Ernie often: trinkets, knick-knacks and curios from travels halfway around the world adorned every conceivable surface, much like the chaotic but precious clutter that littered his own home. It was a treat to come here and chew the fat, discuss the news of the day in the evening and then, when the dusk of evening caused dark shadows to form in the corners of the shelves, to take one of those curious items in hand, wipe away traces of dust and tease the story of its origins gently from Ernie.

"A mind as bright as yours is like a sponge," Ernie continued, distracting Gerald from his thoughts, "ready and keen to soak up every little tit bit of information that comes across it and if you practise, practise and practise again, you'll have the world at your fingertips."

With all the recent changes in his life, Gerald felt as if he already did, but he held his peace a little longer as he knew from their previous talks that Ernie would not be silenced or swayed from his topic until he was done. A good job the man had a manner of speaking that was engaging and held his interest, for their little chats, as Ernie put it, had a habit of running on for a broad chunk of time. Nodding in the right places and taking note of the current subject, Gerald was pleased when at last the stream of words slowed down and Ernie took a seat at the large wooden desk, leather covered, opposite him.

"Well? I asked you a question, man! What do you know of auras? Do you know how to see them for yourself?"

Leaning back in his chair, Gerald hooked one foot over the opposite knee and confessed he knew very little. He was surprised that his friend suddenly opened the subject up for conversation so soon after he had raised the very same thing with Edith. Perhaps she had mentioned it to Ernie. Perhaps the psychic link between them all was doing its work and the thought had travelled between them through the ether.

"The aura," Gerald began, "is an etheric double of the human body, an energy field, if you like, that extends outwards from the body itself. They can be viewed by sensitives, witches, clairvoyants, mediums and others who describe them as an array of colours hanging in the air around a person."

He glanced at Ernie, who nodded. "Go on, what else?"

"The colours of the aura change, depending on the mood or health of the person concerned. I believe it's possible to learn a great deal about a person by examining their aura in detail, though I admit that seeing them is not something I'm capable of myself."

"Pah!" Ernie scoffed. "Have you even tried? Come." He stood up at once and fetched his jacket from the back of his chair, shrugged himself into it and walked out without a second glance back to Gerald, who hurried after him, bewildered.

"Where are we going?"

"Hurry up, dear fellow, time is wasting!"

Curiosity was a constant companion these days, Gerald mused, and he traipsed behind Ernie to the hallway downstairs, grabbed his coat from the stand by the door and then swiftly caught up with Ernie who was already half way along the path to the front of his house.

"Close the door behind you, there's a good chap."

Coming from anyone else, the rampant use of 'good chap', 'dear fellow', and the like might irk him but, with Ernie, it was always meant in friendship and as equals, never condescending or haughty. Gerald pulled the door shut and jogged to catch up with Ernie.

There was a hint of rain in the air as they walked, quite swiftly, along Osborne Road and from there to Westridge Road. As the two of them walked at a brisk pace set by Ernie, the threatened rain began to fall in heavy, fat drops and Gerald was glad of his coat, pulling the collar of it up around the back of his neck.

"Where the devil are we going? Can't we get out of this rain before it gets any heavier?"

Ernie said nothing, merely tapped the side of his nose and carried on walking, leaving Gerald no option but tag along and see what became of the day. They soon reached a crossroads where Ernie waited for a break in the traffic and darted over to a pub positioned right on the corner and made his way inside. Was he being deliberately annoying? This was supposed to be a scheduled day of study and Ernie had promised to school him in the practicalities and techniques of magic, yet here he was eager for a pint of beer instead.

The pub's heavy wooden door creaked open a fraction and Ernie's head appeared in the gap and he called across the street. "Aren't you coming in, I thought you wanted to get out of the rain?"

He had to admit that he wasn't entirely averse to the idea of a beverage, though his preferred choice would be a strong cup of tea with generous helpings of milk and sugar rather than a beer, and the rain was likely to grow much worse, judging by the dark skies, so he made a dash over the road and pulled open the heavy wooden door to join Ernie. The least the impulsive man could do was to furnish Gerald with a nice hot cup of tea while they talked.

After a while of sitting quietly with Ernie, each of them nursing their drinks and keeping their thoughts to themselves, it was clear that there was not going to be much in the way of conversation and Gerald's mind wandered, as it often did, towards the people around him.

He had a habit, perhaps a bad one, perhaps not, of watching strangers and musing to himself about them. If he saw a lady walking alone with her head looking down, he wondered if she was having serious, melancholic thoughts of a dying relative, or if she had been recently jilted and that was the cause of her solemn face. An older man with a young woman on his arm might well be her father, but he could equally be stepping out with her, unbeknown to the chap's poor wife. Gerald couldn't help himself as he looked about the place for somebody interesting to watch, if for no other reason than Ernie was keeping his own counsel and the silence was driving him to distraction. He was particularly interested in the couple seated to his left, squirreled away in a dark corner of the Rose and Crown.

The man was young-looking, in his mid-twenties Gerald estimated, with dark, short-cropped hair and his companion was a fair-haired woman of similar age. Leaning towards the woman across the table, the young man was talking earnestly in hushed tones but from the look of it, the lady was adamantly against whatever he seemed to be proposing. Arms folded and legs crossed beneath the table, a scowl crossed her brow and she stood up swiftly, snatched up her clutch bag and over-coat and sniffed loudly as she walked briskly out of the pub. The gentleman had surely just been rejected, for the look on his face was nearly unbearable and Gerald turned away, embarrassed for the poor chap and not wanting to be caught gawking and making the man feel worse.

A foot kicked him under the table and Ernie whispered. "At last, something to observe. What do you make of that?"

"I suppose his girl has turned him down for some reason."

"What makes you think so?"

"It's obvious, isn't it?" Gerald answered. "Not only did the young woman leave in a hurry, he looks utterly blue."

"Exactly!" Ernie put down his glass and clapped his hands delightedly. "Look again, use your senses this time. Look beyond the physical expressions or mannerisms. Don't just look with your eyes: use your perception, Gerald. Your intuitions. Why did you say he looks blue?"

"Well, he - I suppose I just..." Gerald couldn't put his finger on it, other than the obvious miserable look on the man's face, and so he did as Ernie suggested and tried to observe not only with his eyes, but with his senses, his mind's eye. As he watched, the man picked up a newspaper, straightened the pages and settled to read, but Gerald noticed that his fingers were trembling slightly, his jaw clenched. The encounter with the young lady had clearly upset him.

No, that wouldn't do at all. Gerald chided himself: he still was looking with his eyes. Open your mind, you fool! What do you sense? Gerald relaxed his eyes, letting his vision become hazy and unfocused, and then he saw it.

"What the devil?" He turned to Ernie in astonishment, hoping for confirmation of what he was experiencing, but Ernie stayed still and kept his mouth closed. Gerald looked at the young man again. The newspaper now laid on the table, the man's arms were folded as he sat back in his chair, head hanging miserably low. Behind him the walls were dark, little light entering this secluded corner of the old building with its low ceilings and dark, panelled walls, and against that darkness Gerald could see a vague tinge of dark blue all around the forlorn chap.

It looked almost as if he were surrounded by a cloud, perhaps, or a faint mist, that shrouded him from head to toe. No, not a mist, he could not quite see it clearly enough to determine the shape of it. Gerald half-closed his eyes again, to see if that made a difference and sure enough, the colour did appear to take a form

"I feel as if my eyes have just opened for the first time. I can see it, Ernie, I can see it!" Excited at his discovery, Gerald laughed out loud and slapped his hands on the table and every person in the place turned around to see what all the fuss was about. "I can see it!'

"Pipe down, Gerald; everyone is looking." Ernie smiled fondly and reached over, patting Gerald on the shoulder.

"What of it? I have never much cared for what other people think of me and I don't intend to start worrying about it now," Gerald said. "Let them think what they like."

"Can you do it again, do you think?'

Gerald slowed his breathing down with deliberate deep breaths and settled back as comfortably as he could in the wooden chair with its high back and hard seat and he let his eyes relax and recapture that lazy, hazy focus. Not only was the sad looking man still bathed in a blue tinge of light, it was clearer now, more defined, and Gerald knew without a doubt that this was the man's aura. No wonder, he thought, that we use the expression of feeling blue for moments of sadness and melancholy.

It dawned on him that Ernie had brought him here very deliberately and he wondered aloud what exactly it was about the circumstances here that facilitated his ability to see the young man's aura so clearly.

"It's a reasonably dark environment," Ernie explained, "and for a beginner like yourself, the aura is best seen against a darkened background. Some folk reckon that a white background is better, but trust me, I've seen auras since I was - oh, I don't know how young - and a dark, somewhat gloomy background seems to do the trick more often than not. Add to that the fact that people come to places like this to either commiserate or celebrate something, their emotions are heightened, again contributing to the visibility of the aura."

"You're a scoundrel." Gerald said. "You could have told me."

"That's true enough," Ernie admitted, "but don't you appreciate it even more for finding it out for yourself?"

Gerald laughed, the sound piercing the atmosphere and several of the pub's patrons turned to look across at the source of such humour in these terrible times. He smiled at the onlookers, who returned their gaze to their companions with mild expressions of embarrassment. Ernie may have been concerned about anyone overhearing their esoteric talk, but for himself, he was pleased that his initial forays into the art of seeing the aura had lifted the mood and brought to others a little of the joy he felt himself, even if they couldn't begin to guess the reason for his laughter.

~ EIGHT ~

No More Marmalade Tarts

Thursday 28th September 1939

A few minutes before the appointed time, as was his custom, Gerald rang the doorbell at Theano. Edith opened the door to let him in. She was impeccably dressed, hair pinned back into tidy curls that framed her face. He should have worn trousers, he supposed, but the autumn weather was mild and his shorts were far more comfortable. He had trimmed his moustache and run a comb through his unruly hair, however, so that would have to do.

"Go into the sitting room, Gerald. I'm just finishing off something. I'll be with you shortly."

Gerald did as he was told and soon found himself involuntarily perusing the contents of Edith's bookshelves. He only just had time to pick out a book on psychology which caught his attention, when the door opened and in came Edith with a pile of typescript, the pages neatly joined together with treasury tags.

She put it down on a side table and addressed Gerald. "I meant to ask if you'd had a chance to speak with Ernie? He is very knowledgeable."

He nodded and recounted his experience.

"Very good, I trust you were both discreet. Now, after your efforts of last week, I thought I'd better do the same, so I've been working at this more or less full time in between my teaching appointments."

Gerald picked up the pile of paper. Edith was clearly a much better typist than he was, and she'd managed to get some good quality quarto typing paper from somewhere.

Edith continued, "I decided that 'A Goddess Arrives' would be the best title. What do you think? No doubt the publishers will let you know if there is anything they're not happy with. You have got a publisher, haven't you, Gerald?"

"Oh, yes. I've signed the contract. I've had to pay quite a lot of the costs involved, but that, I gather, is normal."

Edith looked at him quizzically. "Is it Gerald?" she replied, "Is it really?"

Edith sat herself down opposite Gerald. "It was a mammoth job correcting the spelling and grammar, taking far longer than I expected. I've had a good look at the story and, while it's not at all bad, I think the structure could be improved with some scenes in a different order, so that the narrative flows better. I've re-written whole sections and I took the liberty to introduce some additional scenes, or parts of scenes. You might call them 'fragments', I suppose."

At this, Gerald scoffed and spluttered his tea. "Not necessary, surely? I feel the book is complete as it is."

"May I remind you that you asked for my opinion and advice? Do feel free to remove them if you wish. They were only intended to be helpful. It's your book, after all, and the final decision must be yours. As far as I'm concerned, it's ready to be sent off to the publishers, though I'm afraid they may consider it too long. If they do, I can suggest some passages that could, with benefit, be deleted. But, Gerald, I must say that over all I think it's a very good book. And ..." she paused for a second "... as a result I've baked some more marmalade tarts."

"Oh, Dafo! Thank you so much. Not just for the tarts, but all the work you've done on the book. I really am so grateful. I shall dedicate the book to you."

"Absolutely not, Gerald! I can't afford to be associated with such things in public. It wouldn't do my professional practice any good, and I rely on that for my livelihood."

Edith left the room, leaving Gerald in a quandary. He had a feeling she would not think much of his ideas for another book. He was pondering on the best way of broaching the subject when Edith came in with a tray full of tea things and a large plate of marmalade tarts.

While Edith was pouring the tea, Gerald introduced the matter that he had been pondering over.

"Edith, what would you say if I were to write a factual book on witchcraft today? It seems a shame that such a wonderful thing should be hidden away. I'm sure there would be a lot of people interested."

Edith stopped mid-pour and put down the teapot. "Gerald," she said, in her most school-mistressy voice, "don't you remember the oath you took? You must not reveal anything about the Craft. I simply cannot afford to be associated with the author of a book about witchcraft! You know how these rumours spread. If it were known or suspected locally that I was a witch, then every time someone's chickens died or a child became sick, I should be blamed."

"But there's no persecution these days!"

"Isn't there? I'm not so sure. We are at war, Gerald, people are suspicious of the slightest little things already, seeing spies on every street corner or watching for unusual activity. My neighbour is already too nosey for her own good and I cannot risk being associated with anything out of the ordinary. It's one thing to have been involved with the Ashrama, which had the respectability of theatre and performance, it's quite something else to be known as a witch. No, I can't approve of your ideas for such a book. Witchcraft doesn't pay for broken windows." She folded her arms and crossed her legs neatly at the ankles; clearly, she would not be budged on the matter.

Gerald accepted that he would get no further in persuading Edith and suspected that it would take him quite a while to convince her otherwise. His hand stretched out almost unconsciously towards the plate of marmalade tarts.

"No, Gerald! No marmalade tarts until you promise me you will go no further with this ridiculous idea."

"All right, Dafo, if you insist." Gerald replied reluctantly and took a marmalade tart before they could be withdrawn. Duly chastised, he took his leave and started his bike ride back to Southridge, thoughts of their little dispute crowding his mind.

~ NINE ~

A Witches' Circle

Friday 29th September 1939

Gerald had been left feeling chastened and foolish after his recent visit with Edith, during which he had unwittingly upset her. He ought to have known she would not like his ideas of writing about the magical arts in detail. She seemed to have forgiven him, however, and had invited him to take part in a magical healing ritual for an acquaintance of young Rosanne's. The girl, Alice, had a sprained ankle that was taking its time to get better.

He stood by, watching for now, as his companions, for Ernie and Susie joined them, busied themselves with the preparations; taking herbs and resins out of jars to mix into a cloudy incense, lighting candles, placing the working tools, mainly wooden wands in a variety of lengths, a sword and a cluster of gleaming knives, in what seemed to him to be very careful and precise positions on the altar. Gerald had been researching exactly this sort of ritual for years, decades even, but even so he felt out of his depth though he was, naturally, determined not to show it. Perhaps this was the way they had all felt themselves on their first few times in the circle. A hapless bystander trying desperately to please everyone and join in, while just as desperately trying not to get in the way or to say the wrong thing. All at once, at some unseen signal, the witches started to undress. Shoes, shirts, dresses and underwear were either strewn haphazardly or neatly folded and placed on chairs. Gerald at least knew how to join in with that and he disrobed, placing his clothes tidily on the top of an ottoman he spied sitting neatly in one corner of the room.

Noticing that two of the altar candles had gone out, he looked quickly around, spied a box of matches, struck one and re-lit the candles, the flames sparking back to life and casting shadows of the Horned God statue onto the wall behind the altar. He couldn't resist a small chuckle when he realised the shadow had a distinctly phallic shape and the others joined in with good humour.

Standing in silence now, the witches drew themselves into a small circle in the centre of the room, shoulder to shoulder, eyes closed. Gerald did likewise and became aware of the deep, rhythmic sound of everyone breathing in time with each other. His own breath matched it and a gentle, subtle something came over him. A sense of oneness, fullness, connection. Indescribable. This, he realised, as the witches went on with the formality of casting the circle, is the reason it's called a mystery tradition.

The witch motioned for the group to hold hands and the ghost of a smile played on her lips as they caught each other's eyes for a brief moment and then, with a sudden speed, she led them deosil, sunwise, round the circle and began to chant.

> "Eko, eko, Azarak
> Eko, eko, Zomelak..."

The chanting grew louder, the dancing quicker and a buzzing, tingling sensation coursed through his very blood, and still they danced the circle round, spinning, calling, dancing, chanting, and then, when he thought it could go on no longer or he would surely burst with energy, the last cry of words went up with a loud wail, hands raised high in the centre of the circle, the witches stopped abruptly. Breathing hard, Gerald felt elated, his heart racing, exhilarated.

Now the High Priestess walked slowly to the altar, took up her small, personal knife, a gleaming athame engraved with occult sigils, and held it over the small cloth doll that had been placed on the altar before the rite began.

With the doll in the centre of their little circle, the witches held their hands over it, willing it to be filled with healing energy.

"Let Alice be healed, all health restored to her body and soul, we will it so and so it shall be, by the might of the Goddess. Blessed be!"

Gerald echoed the traditional words with the rest of the small group and willed for the young lady the little cloth doll represented to be healed and whole. He visualised her in his mind's eye, whole, healthy and full of life, just as the witch had instructed him to.

Now all he had to do was wait for word from the witch in the coming days to hear if the spell had worked.

~ TEN ~

What Does Ernie Know?

Saturday 28th October 1939

"It is such a beautiful day, it seems quite a shame to be sitting indoors with these old dears for company instead of strolling along the sea-front taking in the fresh air." Edith looked out of the window, taking in the bright sun, the foliage outside dancing in the light breeze that flurried in from the sea and the puffs of white clouds sailing slowly across the sky.

"Not that we would be able to do that today, or any time soon, most likely. The view over the beach is spoiled rotten by the troops making a start on the sea defences. They are whipping it up rather quickly." Susie replied, sounding slightly miserable about it.

"And with good reason," Edith said, "but it does seem a pity we can't enjoy the sun while it lasts. Instead of walking off a leisurely lunch and taking in the sea air, here we are."

"We've nothing to complain about compared to some though," her companion replied, "in any case, it was you who talked me into coming here. I've never been much of a one for handicrafts. I blame you entirely."

"I haven't the foggiest idea if your work is supposed to be a sock or a hat and therefore I absolutely refuse any and all responsibility. You can take the blame if we have our offerings thrown back at us, Susie."

Edith picked up the offending project that Susie was making a hash of, holding it as if it might explode at any minute. If she managed to finish it, it would join a growing pile of hats, gloves, socks and balaclavas, all of them knitted or crocheted by local women working under the patronage of Violet Stuart Wortley, Lady of Highcliffe Castle. The garments, hand-knitted in thick strands of brown, navy, green and black, were not going to go far if the reports she'd heard that morning were correct. Twenty thousand men called to arms and signed up, on top those already enlisted and overseas. Brave and bold, young and courageous, twenty thousand men, and some of them barely sixteen, all ready to fight for their country. And here I sit, knitting those soldiers a warm piece of clothing while they face the unknown terrors of the battlegrounds. How inadequate of me. How very mundane and worthless. She must have spoken that last thought out loud, for Susie looked at her quizzically.

Edith poured them both another cup of tea, weak and pale with little sugar or milk to taste and little in the way of tea either, for that matter, and silently cursed her ration book. She picked up a ball of navy wool, ready to start casting on stitches to make yet another balaclava with matching gloves. The hall was full of polite chatter and the gentle clicking of metal against metal as the gathering of ladies gossiped while picking up stitches to do their bit.

"Thank you for joining us, ladies." A volunteer joined them, an older woman with fly-away wisps of grey hair, who looked as if the faintest breeze would blow her right over, and who took a closer look at the piece of knitting that Susie was working on.

"I say, what is that you're making, dear? Looks like a cross between a balaclava and a three-fingered glove. Well, not to worry, you'll soon get the hang of it, I'm sure. I was a fine knitter and seamstress in my day, though you'd be hard pressed to believe it now, with my hands full of arthritic lumps as they are these days." She held a cardboard box into which she placed the finished items and, by the look of it, the box was starting to get heavy.

"It's still your day." Susie smiled and patted the seat of the vacant chair beside her, inviting the woman to sit with them for a time. "Here, take the weight off your feet for a few minutes."

The woman nodded gratefully and put down the box. "Thank you, that's very kind of you. Just a drop of milk and spare the sugar."

Edith tried not to wrinkle her nose at the taste of the weak tea as they made small talk with the woman. Mrs Graves had recently retired to Walkford with her husband for the sea air and would be sitting in the sun enjoying it right at this very minute, if not for the wretched war.

"And so soon after the last one, barely recovered from one onslaught and here we are again for round two. Never mind, my dears," Their elderly companion finished her tea and picked up her box. "We all do our bit, don't we?"

"Let me take that for you." Susie offered to carry the box to the other end of the hall, where another volunteer was busy sorting things into piles.

"Thank you, but it's not carrying things I struggle with, Susan," Mrs Graves insisted, "just the fine detail my hands can't manage these days."

"It's all very well and good making these balaclavas and gloves for our troops, Susie," Edith muttered once the elderly lady was out of ear-shot, "but there really ought to be something more we could do. I refuse, Susie, I absolutely refuse to do nothing but sit around with a pair of knitting needles or a crochet hook when surely there is real work that needs to be done."

"Why does everyone assume I'm a Susan? I'm damn well ..."

"Mind your language, please." The teacher in Edith came out with these things automatically, whether she wanted to say them or not.

"Don't scold me, Edith, I'm not one of your students." Susie huffed. "There are plenty of other ways we could be helping out, I'm sure."

Edith folded her arms in annoyance and glanced momentarily through the window where a gathering of dull grey clouds threatened to disturb the calm weather. No birds flying today, not even the gulls whose repertoire of cawing screeches so often assaulted one's ears this close to the sea. Was the disturbance of war affecting even the birds, now? Were they too falling prey to the atmosphere of tense anticipation and worry that bothered the country?

"If that is what you think then please, go ahead and enlighten me, because I am sick to my bones of half-hearted gestures. I'm neither young enough or fit enough to be working on the land from dusk till dawn as some women are doing. Go ahead, Susan," she used the moniker deliberately, not able to help herself from stirring things up a little, "you tell me. What worthwhile task is a person in my position capable of that would bring any tangible benefit to our troops, to our country, in the face of such a horrific enemy?"

Eyes darting around the room, Susie shook her head briskly from side to side.

Susie leaned forward and, whispering to make sure she wouldn't be overhead, she said, "Not here, I'll tell you later."

Edith raised an eyebrow in curiosity. Susie continued, "Ernie and I are both volunteers for the A.R.P., and I shall tell you, it's a damn - sorry - a dashed sight more exciting than getting balls of wool into a muddle."

Edith took the tangle of wool that Susie had been struggling with, her deft fingers unpicking the knots and bumps that had formed.

"Wandering the streets at night shouting 'lights out' until the small hours of the morning come rain or shine is not my idea of fun."

"It isn't supposed to be fun. There is a lot more to it than that, you know. Besides, there may be other things we can do, things that, hang on." She stopped the conversation short as Mrs Graves, the talkative volunteer came by, carrying an armful of finished garments. "I can't say any more, not here."

"I hope you're not thinking of something illegal? Or dangerous? Perhaps you had better not tell me at all, I suspect my neighbour thinks Gerald and I are - carrying on - as it is, I don't want any more gossip being slung around."

"All I will say for now is that Ernie knows things." Susie leaned in towards Edith, her voice barely more than a whisper, eyes darting around to see if anyone was listening in. "People like us, people with our particular interests, shall we say, have a way of making things happen. Look, I really must dash, it's past two already. I have a return train ticket back to Southampton and don't want to be late."

"You can't leave me hanging like this. What does Ernie know? It's unfair of you not to tell me."

"We'll speak of it again, very soon. Ask Ernie when you have the chance, he will be able to tell you more about it than I."

With that, Susie swiftly cleared away the odd socks, knitting needles and balls of wool she had been toying with, and left Edith sitting among the old dears, none the wiser.

Air Raid Precautions Handbook No. 8

A Warden's Duties in War

In time of war, an air raid warden should regard himself first and foremost as a member of the public chosen and trained to be a leader of his fellow-citizens and, with them and for them, to do the right thing in any emergency.

The keynotes of his conduct should be **courage and presence of mind.**

His duty at his post will be only when a raid is threatened, and he should go there immediately he hears the Warning signal (if he has not been warned to do so before). and see that his equipment is there. He should put on his armlet, and his steel helmet with its anti-gas curtain and the eye-shield, and carry his Civilian Duty respirator. He should also put a whistle in his pocket.

The Senior Warden or Second Warden at the post will take charge.

If wardens come on duty **before the Action Warning is given**, it will be best for them to remain at the post. Remember that until the Action Warning the public are expected to continue their ordinary occupations without interruption. See Section 8.

When the Warning signal is heard, or when the Action Warning is received at the post by telephone from headquarters, the public duty of the wardens begins. **One warden will always remain at the post**, to be ready to answer the telephone and send reports. The others will patrol the sector.

The streets should be cleared. People not within reach of home (that is, who cannot get there in 5 minutes) should be directed to the nearest public shelter, or other refuge accommodation.

~ ELEVEN ~

The Night Patrol

Saturday 25th November 1939

It was very late in the evening when Gerald and Edith, who had contrived their shift on the rota to coincide, thus allowing them to walk their allotted route with each other, spied a large detached house, set back from the road slightly, with not only one or two, but all of its windows ablaze with light. They had called out to no avail and it was not until they spoke to the house-holder that the problem was dealt with.

"What's all this bother about?" A balding man with a thin moustache answered the knock at the door and immediately looked past Edith to Gerald.

"You must put your lights out, Sir." Edith said. Susie had been right, volunteering made her feel she was contributing, and this was what she had signed up for, but she did wish that people would make it a little easier sometimes.

"Says who, eh?" The man looked at her sternly. He was taller than her by five or six inches and she felt quite sure his expression was one of disdain. He looked again at Gerald, standing slightly behind Edith.

A large white 'W' stood out clearly on the front of their helmets and the starchy, scratchy uniforms marked them out as Air Raid Precaution wardens. It should not have been necessary to identify themselves, thought Edith. Besides, surely any citizen spotting this would raise the matter with the house-holder, not only those with a modicum of authority?

"My colleague and I are air raid protection wardens, Sir," Gerald told him, "and as she has already explained, we must insist you put out your lights or cover your windows."

The man huffed audibly, nodded with reluctance and turned to go back inside, muttering as he did so. They caught only a fragment of what he said as they retreated but Edith couldn't help being annoyed. He might well be hosting a dinner party, lucky for him, but that did not excuse him from breaking the rules and risking the safety not only of those in the house, but the lives of everyone for miles around.

"Imagine how he would feel if it was his fault the street was spotted from the air. I hope he will think twice in future." Gerald said, and they continued their patrol.

It was close to midnight and the lanes and roads were quite deserted by now, all sensible people tucked up in bed for the night. Edith and Gerald had been walking for hours now and it was high time they had a break for a cup of tea to keep them going, in her opinion. Not Gerald though. She looked up at him, striding beside her in comfortable silence. A man of action, she thought, he had a determination to see things through and get the job done.

And thank goodness for that, she mused, as otherwise he would never get that book of his published.

"Does it come easily to you?" she asked him. He looked at her blankly. "Writing, I mean, your book, and the research for it."

"Sometimes the words flow out of me like a river but at other times, usually when I am distracted by something else or if I'm tired, it can be hard to get started. Once I get going though, I could sit at my desk all day and night, rushing through the story to reach the exciting parts."

"I should imagine that makes your fingers cramp after a time. You really must invest in a typewriter of your own, Gerald, it would be so much quicker - not to say neater."

"I say, you take that back. My writing is quite neat enough for me."

"Barely legible, if you ask me." She smiled up at him, hoping her expression was clear enough in the dark for him to see that she was teasing him.

"Now, now, Dafo." He replied. Despite the darkness of the night, and without street lamps, car head-lights or the chink of light from windows, it was very dark, yet there was a visible twinkle in his eye. "One could say a few things about you in return, but one would not stoop to such comments in front of a lady."

Edith stopped, a pace or two in front of him, and folded her arms across her chest, eyeing him beadily. "This lady is quite able to take criticism, I shall have you know."

Gerald inclined his head, seemed to think about this for a moment, nodded twice and continued walking, carefully crossing the junction that marked their half-way point. She followed, as he'd known she would.

"Well, in that case, I do think you could be a little more light-hearted at times."

"What do you mean? I am light-hearted."

"On the surface, I would agree, but there are times when you seem distracted - worried, I suppose - and I want you to know you can trust me, Edith, if you wanted to talk about it."

Edith sighed. Annoyingly, he was right. Now she was glad of the night, for the shadows masked the frown that creased her brow. "It's Rosanne and Tommy. I do hope she's doing the right thing. She has the whole world in front of her and yet she is determined to carry on with him and settle down. I would positively hate to see her unhappy in a few years' time, with a broken marriage behind her and children to raise on her own, as I have had to do these last years."

"That's an understandable concern," he said. "She has a bright mind, though, and he seems a likeable fellow. I'm sure that she..."

"It isn't only that, of course." Edith continued as if Gerald hadn't spoken. "It's this blasted war. Shouting at folk to keep to the rules, not knowing when the Germans are going to invade, the threat of it all hanging over our heads and now Rosanne is due to be married and how shall I make her cake with so little sugar and who knows if I will have enough eggs? I can't get any material for a dress for love nor money and there's all kinds of things she will have to do without." Now that she had started to confide in Gerald, this dear man who had come into her life too late to do anything about it, she couldn't stop.

"Two of her friends have taken up positions as land-girls, because with all the men-folk called to arms, farmers run the risk of produce rotting in the ground where it sits. Alice, her friend with the ankle, she's one of them. Her ankle did improve, by the way, I think I told you that, didn't I? My beautiful roses are withering because I haven't the time to tend them, I have been too busy planting potatoes and turnips instead, not that my little garden is large enough to be an allotment - I would move to a bigger house if only I could afford it. Oh, and let's not forget the children carrying around their gas-masks every day. Young George Oscott, one of my pupils, told me that his mother has a suitcase packed ready-and-waiting by the front door, in case they should have to flee in the middle of the night. He thinks it's exciting, Gerald, as though they were preparing for a holiday! I can't bear it, I simply can't!"

Edith had come to the end of her raving. She burst into tears, looking away from Gerald but he caught her arm gently and there, standing at the crossroads at Sea Corner, the very centre of Highcliffe, in the stillness and quiet of the night, he pulled her into his arms, hugged her in a warm embrace. The rim of her helmet was digging into his shoulder but still she pressed against him for comfort. For a minute or an hour, she couldn't tell how long, she remained safe in his arms while she regained her composure and recovered from her fit of tears.

Feeling safer with his arms around her, she lifted her head and looked up into his kind eyes. The ends of his moustache brushed over her skin as he placed a gentle, quick kiss upon her cheek. She moved away, breaking their embrace, and began to walk slowly. His footsteps followed her, and the moment passed.

The threat of invasion on the English coast had been on everybody's mind for weeks and things showed no sign of calming down. Only a day or two ago, Gerald himself had shivered with cold dread when he listened to the latest reports on his wireless. Norway and Denmark had been attacked and it was surely only a matter of time before the same thing happened here. There was little wonder Edith was upset.

Gerald caught up with her and held her arm. "There now, it will be all right." He said simply.

"Will it?" Her eyes wide, she drew away slightly and looked into his eyes. "Will it?"

Although he wanted to reassure her, Gerald could not answer that. Nobody could.

~ TWELVE ~

A Book Arrives

Monday 18th December 1939

Gerald was up bright and early that Monday morning. He was expecting a package by special delivery and he was finishing off his breakfast and becoming increasingly agitated until the sound of the doorbell caused him to jump out of his chair, knocking his knee in the process. He had no time for his usual expletives, however, but made straight for the front door.

On opening it, he was greeted by a delivery man holding a large, heavy cardboard box, which he put down on the step as Gerald opened the door.

"Mr. Gardner?"

"Dr. Gardner, actually."

"Well, I've a special delivery for you. Can you sign here please?

Gerald did so and watched to make sure the delivery man closed the gate behind him before carrying the box into the house.

He undid the string tied around the box, opened the cardboard flaps and removed wodges of packing paper to reveal printed copies of his new book, "A Goddess Arrives", fresh from the printers. He picked a copy out and, holding it in his hands, admired it. It was a thick book, 382 pages long. It had a specially drawn dust jacket, which had come out very well, and a fine green cover with gold lettering.

If he was honest with himself, it had cost quite a lot of money. Not only had he paid the costs of production, but he had paid extra to make sure the book was finished and delivered by today, which was Edith's fifty-second birthday. He hoped the gift of a book and another present would go some way to lifting the gloomy mood that had settled over Edith these last few months. It pained him to see his friend so upset and worried.

He quickly put a few items in his haversack and started the familiar cycle trip to Dennistoun Avenue. As soon as Edith opened the door, Gerald wished her a Happy Birthday and presented her with a copy of his new book.

"These only came this morning and I haven't even had time to wrap it. Do you like it? It looks nice, doesn't it? Feel the covers! Look at the gold lettering on the spine!"

"It looks lovely, but do come in, won't you? I was just about to have elevenses. I thought you might be round, so I baked some marmalade tarts, just in case. Go through."

"I am glad that you like the book, I'm incredibly satisfied with it." said Gerald, after they were both seated and he had just finished his first marmalade tart of the day. "Now, here is your proper birthday present."

He handed her a small item wrapped in what looked like a spare piece of William Morris wallpaper and tied with a gold ribbon with not inconsiderable skill. It had a luggage-type label with, 'For Dafo on her Birthday, much love, Gerald xxx', written in his neatest handwriting.

Edith opened it and revealed a semi-circular object, much in the form of a cycle-clip but wider, and made of what looked like silver. There was a strange pattern engraved into it that looked like an inscription in an unknown language.

"Dear Gerald, that looks marvellous. But whatever is it? And where did you get it?"

"Well, it's a bracelet, more properly called a cuff, I believe. I made it for you myself. You know I've got a little workshop up in the attic. Over the years, I've accumulated quite a lot of metal-working skills, which I honed to a fine art when I was in Ceylon.

If a piece of machinery broke down there was no-one to mend it and to order a spare part from Colombo took days, if not weeks. Even longer if it had to be ordered from Birmingham. I got into the habit of making spare parts on the small forge we had on the plantation. So, I thought I'd have a go at the bracelet for you. I ordered some sheet silver and once that arrived it really didn't take too long."

Edith took the bracelet and put it on her wrist, sliding it up her arm until it was tight.

"Well, I think it's delightful, but what are the characters inscribed on it?

"Oh, that just says 'Dafo' in the Theban alphabet, Cornelius Agrippa's private code. Now, if you have no other plans for the day, why not visit a friend of mine with me? I'm taking a copy of the book to him and I think you would rather like him."

Edith nodded and Gerald grinned happily. Whether it was her birthday or his gifts that improved her mood, he was glad she seemed to be in brighter spirits today and they set off to visit Walter Forder.

"The name's familiar. How do you know him?"

"Walter and I met a while back at the Ashrama, you have probably seen him there yourself at one time or another, writing a report on some dramatic enterprise or another. He is the editor of the Christchurch Times."

"That's right, I have met him, though only in passing. Now here you are, with your brand new book in hand." She laughed at him and playfully batted his arm. "Let me guess, Mr Forder is about to receive a copy of his own to review for the newspaper."

"Come along with me, why don't you? See what he makes of it for yourself. I thought he might enjoy it and if he happens to place a positive review in the paper, I shan't object."

And, thought Gerald, taking her arm as they walked, meeting Walter would be just the kind of thing she needed to keep her going in these dark times.

Walter turned out to be a gracious host, supplying his visitors with ample refreshments, much to Gerald's delight. With pride, Gerald presented Walter with his book and barely managed to curb his excitement as Walter sang its praises. Gerald beamed and clapped his hands together with excitement.

"I'd be thrilled to review it for the paper. Rather nice, isn't it?" Walter spotted Edith keenly admiring an ornate oak bookcase.

"Yes, though I was really interested in the books, Walter, not the case itself."

The two men exchanged a brief, knowing glance and Walter smiled, looking at the eclectic range of books. "I thought as much. We have similar interests in the esoteric, I gather, although I am sure your knowledge far exceeds my own."

A scratching sound distracted Walter and he went through the drawing room to the kitchen where he opened the door to let in a small tabby cat.

"Gerald tells me you're a gardener, is that right? Would you like to see my efforts?"

Walter led them out into his garden and chatted happily with Edith about the various flowers, plants and shrubs that lay dormant in the winter soil.

"You must come again when the peonies are in bloom. I have several varieties, you see, and they do make a splendid show."

Edith said she would like that very much and, with a sigh that very much spoke of his disinterest in peonies, Gerald intruded on their conversation.

"I say, look at the time." He realised this was not very subtle and tried to backtrack. After all, he had commandeered most of the conversation until now, focused as he was on Walter's enthusiasm for his new book. "I only mean that..."

"No, you're quite right, Gerald. I have a habit of rambling, I'm afraid." Walter turned to Edith with a sheepish look on his face. "I won't keep you any longer, my dear. We never did have a chance to discuss those books, so I hope to see you again before too long."

"I'm sure our paths will cross again soon." Edith smiled as they took their leave and linked arms with Gerald as they walked along.

He patted her hand, as he seemed to more often these days, and reminded her that not every conversation had to revolve around the mystical and magical.

"That's true," Edith agreed, "but aren't those conversations the best kind?"

~ THIRTEEN ~

A Grand Yarn

Saturday 27th January 1940

Though the winter had begun with rain and wind, the weather today was cold, but not unpleasantly so, and Gerald propped his bicycle against the wall at the side of the driveway at Edith's home on Dennistoun Avenue, and rang the bell. He waited impatiently for her to open the door.

Almost before she had a chance to say good-morning, he waved the newspaper he had brought with him in front of her face and then marched straight into the lounge, whereupon he sat down and spread the paper, the Christchurch Times, open over his lap.

"I'm very pleased to find you at home, Edith, there is something I am keen to show you."

"Hello to you too, Gerald. Do come in, won't you?" Edith sat across the room from him and as he looked up from the newspaper, he noticed a somewhat bemused expression on her face.

"What? Oh yes, I apologise for being abrupt, but as you might gather, I am rather eager for you to see this. Now let me find it ..." He thumbed through the pages until he found what he was looking for and then, with an air of reverence, he started to pass the paper across to her.

Edith reached for it but, Gerald snatched it away. "No, I shall read it out to you."

"Is this about the rationing? I hope it helps to make things go around a little more fairly. No eggs yesterday, not one. Luckily one of my neighbours keeps a couple of hens so I was able to swap some eggs for a bottle of my elderberry vinegar."

"Oh, that. No," he replied, "this is something else. Remember I introduced you to Walter Forder? He's written a splendid review of my book." Gerald began reading and Edith sighed, resigning herself to another of his long-winded monologues.

A GODDESS ARRIVES

FINE NEW NOVEL BY HIGHCLIFFE WRITER

A strange story, yet throughout, refreshingly strange, scholarly and bearing with it the imprint of a fine imagination, "A Goddess Arrives" carries with it locally an added interest, since its author is a Highcliffe resident.

MAIDEN LANE TO ANCIENT CYPRUS

To select a theme built upon re-incarnation and to swing the story back and forth between Maiden Lane, London, that dingy little thoroughfare so steeped in Victorian theatrical history and ancient Cyprus of 1450., was surely some undertaking. But to evolve a thrilling novel out of the theme, playing with history and fact, with all the skill of a Rider Haggard, makes it little short of a masterpiece.

THE TROJAN WARS

From the Trojan Wars with finely conceived imaginings as to how their cumbersome engines of attack were made, to a sordid triangular drama in a gloomy flat in London of to-day, and back again from a picture of a man lying still as death in catalepsy to the thrilling recounting of how in ancient Cyprus, Venus Aphrodite, a goddess arrives, is no mean accomplishment, when it is done, as Mr. G. B. Gardner effects it - just like scenes on a revolving stage; it fits and flows.

"The marriage in the Temple of Juske" - one of the chapters - is absolutely of the quality of Haggard. I suppose this impresses because the central character is a wonderful woman. Haggard uses "She" and, Mr. Gardner, Venus Aphrodite.

Magnificently bound, in get up and format and pictorial jacket, faultless, "A Goddess Arrives" is told leisurely (and yet with every line vibrating with interest and thrill) in no less than 382 pages.

It's a grand yarn, and on many occasions a most scholarly and informative narrative, and throughout is a romance that grips. Mr G. B. Gardner may take the unction to his soul that he has accomplished something of which he must be justly proud.

Having finished reading the book review to her, Gerald folded the paper, fingers fumbling. He looked up at Edith, still perched next to him, and wondered what she might be thinking behind those deep eyes, full of soul.

It turned out that she did not say very much at all. She didn't need to - he could see pride written on her face as she moved a little closer.

"Congratulations, Gerald." Her voice was low and she looked deeply into his eyes. "I simply couldn't be happier for you. He's right, you know, it's a very good book."

He was delighted to have such a glowing review and rightly felt rather proud of himself. Still, the book was far more refined and polished than it would have been had he been left entirely to his own devices, to say nothing of his spelling and written grammar, and it would have been wrong of him not to say so.

"It would not have been quite so good without your assistance and I want to thank you wholeheartedly for your efforts."

Edith blushed at this unexpected praise. "Nonsense, you deserve all the glory you get."

ACT TWO

A MAGICAL CALL TO ARMS

Friday 10th May 1940

MANCHESTER GUARDIAN

MR. CHURCHILL PREMIER

MR. CHAMBERLAIN STAYING IN WAR CABINET

Mr. Chamberlain resigned the Premiership last night and has been succeeded by Mr. Winston Churchill, the First Lord of the Admiralty. Following is the official statement: -

The Right Hon. Neville Chamberlain, M.P., resigned the office of Prime Minister and First Lord of the Treasury this evening and the Right Hon. Winston Churchill, C.H., M.P., accepted His Majesty's invitation to fill the position.

The Prime Minister desires that all Ministers should remain at their posts and discharge their functions with full freedom and responsibility while the necessary arrangements for the formation of a new Administration are made.

~ FOURTEEN ~

Gerald's Fishing Finds a Loophole

Monday 20th May 1940

Gerald was on a mission. Major Frederick Merriott Fish was a busy man, having just been appointed Company Commander of the Local Defence Volunteers, but he was exactly the right person, Gerald judged, to be able to help him. Major Fish had been established in a small office in Hengistbury House on the cliff-top in Highcliffe and that was where Gerald now sought him out, keeping his fingers crossed that a solution to his dilemma would be forthcoming.

He knocked on the door, hoping he hadn't left it too late in the day, and was greeted by the Major, an imposing looking man with an air of natural authority about him.

"Good evening, I am sorry for the late appearance, but my name is Gardner - Gerald Brosseau Gardner. If I'm not intruding, I must speak to you urgently about joining the Local Defence Volunteers."

"Well, Mr. Gardner ..."

"It's Dr. Gardner, actually."

"Well, Dr. Gardner, I believe the correct procedure is to register your name at the police station in Highcliffe."

"I tried to do that, but they turned me down!"

Fish gave him the once over and looked puzzled. To all intents and purposes, Gerald was reasonably fit and didn't look over sixty-five by any means.

"On what grounds did they reject you?" Fish put a hand on his chin, shaking his head as he asked the question.

"It seems to be, quite simply, that I was an Air-Raid Warden. My house happens to be the local A.R.P. post. I honestly can't see why I can't be a warden during the raids and a member of the Local Defence Volunteers during the All-Clears."

"Well, I agree with you, but there have been rulings from above, which seem to be based on the belief that the wardens would lose all their best men to the L.D.V. I'm sorry, Dr. Gardner, but I don't see what I can do about the situation. It seems quite clear to me, however much I might not agree with it."

"Can I explain something?" said Gerald, noting that there was a disappointing tone to the Major's voice. As a prime candidate for the task, he could see that Fish was as perplexed by the rules as he was himself. With a little bit of luck, they may be able to find a solution between them.

Fish sighed and invited Gerald back into his office.

"It's getting dark. You really should have blackout curtains fitted by now. As an air-raid warden, I should warn you that you are breaking the law."

"I was about to lock up when you arrived, so it's not normally an issue, but you're quite right. I'll get on with that first thing tomorrow. In the meantime, I have a suggestion to make. Perhaps we could continue our conversation in The Globe?"

"That's a very good idea." Gerald agreed. "I don't drink alcohol, but I am sure I could get a cup of tea there."

"In that case," Fish said, "we can go to the Friar's Rest at Latimers, Mrs. Fordham's house. It's on my way home, in any case."

Gerald was familiar with Latimers, indeed, since his initiation into the witches' circle, had visited several times, as Dorothy Fordham was an acquaintance and friend of several of the witches and had generously offered her spacious home for them to use on special occasions. Luckily, he knew better than to bring up that particular subject and said nothing.

They started wheeling their bicycles in the direction of Station Road, when Gerald decided to ask a question. It had been on his mind for some time that he could be doing more to support the military, outside of his official capacity as a warden. And with a grand collection of armouries in his possession, he knew what kind of support he could offer.

"Look, I don't want you to divulge any Official Secrets, but there have been reports of equipment shortages for troops. Are we also locally short of weapons?"

"I should say that was an accurate assessment of the situation. I haven't yet called the Company together for any training or manoeuvres, but when we do, I doubt if any of them would have much in the way of weaponry, apart from a few pitchforks or garden tools of various descriptions."

Gerald had held a suspicion that this might be the case. "Let me tell you then, that I have been a collector of weapons since I was a boy and have accumulated quite a number that could prove useful in an emergency. I take it that we are in an emergency?"

"I don't think anyone would doubt that." Fish agreed.

"Well, I'll not go into details now, but you might want to come around and see what I've got. The address is Southridge, at the junction of Elphinstone Road and Highland Avenue. Come around tomorrow for elevenses and I'll show you what I've got."

***

Tuesday 21st May 1940

At precisely eleven o'clock the following morning, Major Frederick Fish rolled up to Southridge on his very clean, dark-green bicycle, opened the front gate and leaned his cycle against the wall next to the garage. Gerald spied him from his position on the little wooden balcony that jutted out from the upper floor.

It was one of his favourite spots, looking out over the front garden and onto the quiet road and from where he could watch the world going by. He was pleased to see that Major Fish was punctual and he was quite looking forward to showing off his collection to his new acquaintance.

He made his way downstairs and greeted the Major at the front door. "Major Fish, good to see you. You found the way all right?"

"Oh, yes, that was no problem. I grew up in this area. I acquired my Canadian accent when I served in the Canadian army during the last war. I only came back to this country some two years ago, but not a lot has changed in that time. I'm staying with my family at Burley right now."

"I see, well, do come in. I shall ask Mrs. Fribbens to bring some elevenses. Do you like tea or coffee, by the way? We have both."

"Coffee for preference, but since I've been back in England, I have inevitably started to have a bit of a taste for tea. I am quite keen to have a look at your collection."

"Of course, this way."

He led the way upstairs, where Fish noted one or two ceremonial looking knives mounted on the walls, but it was the suit of armour on the landing that caused him to comment. "I say, that's very striking. It would certainly provide a measure of protection, but at the expense of considerable restriction of movement, I would have thought."

"It wouldn't be very practicable to wear in the event of an invasion, I'm afraid. It's difficult to get into without considerable help. I've only managed it once, it wasn't really my size, and it's difficult even to walk in it properly. No, I have some weapons I'd like you to see. This way."

On the oak-panelled wall was a variety of ornate knives, some curved and highly decorated, all with very thin blades, and each piece was clearly well looked-after and in extremely good condition.

"These are remarkable, Gardner. Did you collect these somewhere in the Far East?"

"Yes, I lived in Ceylon, Borneo and Malaya for thirty-five years. These are examples of the 'kris', the magical Malay weapon, on which I am somewhat of an expert. In fact, I've written a book about them. I'll let you have a copy if you like."

"Thank you, Gardner. But how easy are these knives to use? They look rather fragile."

"They're actually very strong. There's a special technique for making the blades. But the point is that any measure of skill in using them requires years of practice. The idea is that the thin blade can penetrate the body in such a manner that it goes between the ribs, and then can go right to the heart. Doubtful if any of our volunteers would have the necessary skills, however. Come along, Major Fish, I think you will like some of my other pieces."

Gerald led Major Fish into a small back room where dozens upon dozens of relics of various sorts, including pikes and swords, were hanging on the walls. He felt quite a thrill that his weapons were proving to be of such interest and was already starting to imagine them being put to good use.

"What about these, Fish? These could do a lot of damage, I would have thought."

"Well, certainly. I'll bear them in mind. Do you have anything else you think we can use?"

"There's that old Malay cannon in the corner there. To be honest, I've never got it going, but it should be possible to use it. We haven't got any cannon balls, but I imagine we could use anything. Perhaps we could use suitable-sized pebbles off the beach? And we'd need some blasting powder. That's if the thing even works, as I say, I've never tried it. Leave it with me. I'll bring it down to your HQ. But then I'm not supposed to, am I? Be associated with the L.D.V., I mean."

"Don't you worry about that, Gardner," said Major Fish, "I've started looking through the regulations. There's over 500 pages of the T.A. Regulations. That's quite enough material to be able to find at least one loophole. Leave it with me and in the meantime, I shall leave you with a copy of the material I've just received from the Army Council. It's only 29 paragraphs, but does cover the administration of the L.D.V. I've only had a quick look through. You may be able to find something hidden in that which could be of use to us."

"Thank you, I shall read it this evening." Gerald replied, pleased to hear the encouraging news. "Now, I think Mrs. Fribbens should have our elevenses ready for us."

Gerald felt decidedly more cheerful after Major Fish had left Southridge. It would be a satisfying job if he could get the old Malay cannon working, and - the task he was relishing - looking through the regulations for a loophole that would enable him to join the L.D.V., as well as remaining an air-raid warden. He only hoped that after all his showing-off, he really could get the cannon going again - and that he didn't blow himself or anyone else up in the process.

~ FIFTEEN ~

Gerald Tells His Tale and the Masons Tell All

Tuesday 21st May 1940

Gerald was early, arriving for the small meeting at Edith's house. He had barely been let in the door when he reported on his dealings with Major Fish, "Dafo, we've won!"

"Not the war, surely?"

"Fish and I have found the loophole!"

"Calm down, Gerald. Pour yourself a cup of tea, then sit down, relax, and tell me calmly what you are excited about."

Gerald did as he was told and waited, rather impatiently, until Edith joined him.

"Now, Gerald, you may proceed."

"Well, it's a long story ..."

Edith interrupted him: "Are you going to tell the Masons about this?"

"I should jolly well think so!"

"Well, in that case, don't you think you had better wait until they arrive? Otherwise, there's the prospect of having to tell your story twice."

"As long as I can have one of those delicious-looking marmalade tarts while I'm waiting."

At that moment the doorbell rang. Edith went to answer the door and returned, followed by Ernie and Susie Mason, to find Gerald had gone ahead and helped himself to a tart.

Edith stated, "I suppose you all want tea? I seem to be the only one who drinks coffee."

"Well," replied Susie, "Tea is very much an English drink, not like that foreign stuff you seem to like so much!"

"You know very well tea is also an import. Now, what did you have to tell us, Gerald?" She set about drawing the curtains closed as everyone settled in to hear his news.

Gerald needed no encouragement to go straight into his stream of thought. "When Eden announced the formation of Local Defence Volunteers the other day, I decided that I want, indeed, need, to be involved. There was a mighty long queue of people at the police station ready to sign up. By the time I'd got to the head of the queue, they'd had some instruction from somewhere and had designed a form for us to fill in. I filled in the form but they rejected me."

"I can't believe that, surely you are exactly right for the position." Susie said.

"I would have thought so too, but I left my telephone number and early yesterday evening they phoned and told me that A.R.P. wardens are not allowed to be in the Local Defence Volunteers. It was a nice-sounding chap who phoned me and told me about Major Fish, who has been appointed to oversee the L.D.V. in the Highcliffe area working out of a room in Hengistbury House, on the clifftop.

"I immediately went around to see him. Jolly nice chap. We agreed between us to look through the regulations for a loophole and found that any L.D.V. unit may appoint a specialist in any field, such as, for example, armoury, without needing permission from anyone."

Edith's eyes widened as she realised what he must mean. This could be brilliant and effective or completely hare-brained, she wasn't sure which. "Your collection of knives and weapons."

"Exactly," Gerald slapped his knee, his excitement barely containable. "There was an A.R.P. meeting that evening and, when I told them they were very pleased and several of them are now going to apply to join the L.D.V. themselves. Fish and I managed to transport my old Malay cannon to their practice-ground next to Hengistbury House."

Edith put a hand to her mouth in astonishment and concern. A vision floated into her mind of the cannon going horribly wrong and she was relieved when Gerald put her at ease.

"Waste of time, unfortunately, as we could not get it going, though I did experiment with some petrol bombs in old jam jars. They seemed to work although everyone was very rude to me about it. One chap even quoted the Duke of Wellington's saying, 'I don't know if they'll frighten the enemy, but they certainly frighten all on this side'. I was a bit disheartened, to be honest, but they promised they'd use the pikes in my collection."

Gerald fell silent for a few moments. Edith looked at him with some concern. He seemed a little subdued, so she filled in the gap in the conversation, or monologue to be more truthful.

"Well, it's nice to know, as a member of the A.R.P., that I could also join the L.D.V., but to be honest I've no special qualifications and I don't think I could be the slightest bit of use. I'm not as young as I used to be and with the best will in the world, I can't go gallivanting about wielding pitchforks and the like at my age. If only there was some way in which I could use the skills I have, but elocution is hardly a priority when we're facing a wholesale invasion of foreign troops."

"If we were the ones doing the invading, perhaps it might be." Ernie had been quiet until now, but his thoughtful nods had not escaped anybody's attention.

"What do you mean?" Edith asked him.

"Well, infiltration behind enemy lines requires a fair amount of skill in French or German, I would have thought."

"May I remind you that I teach elocution, not languages? No, I hate to say it, but I don't think I can be any use whatever."

"You are also a practitioner in the ancient skills of witchcraft. Why don't you use those skills? Working magically to help ensure that the invasion never happens in the first place. It's been done at least twice before, why not now?"

"What do you mean?"

"I remember my grandfather used to tell me the story of how his father did just that when England was threatened with invasion by Old Boney, back in the early years of last century."

"What did they do?" enquired Edith.

"The whole family went out to Toot Hill, up Romsey way, for a grand sabbat where everyone concentrated their minds on what they wanted to achieve, in this case, to prevent Boney from invading. What they did was an old technique - old even then - where they raised what they called a 'cone of power', a magical entity created by their minds acting together to achieve a common purpose. Those who had the vision saw the cone of power like a cloud hanging in the air over the group."

Edith nodded, thinking on what he had said. "Was this a widely known practice?"

"The technique was old even then and there are rumours it was used against the Spanish Armada in 1588. A terrible storm blew up and the ships in the Armada were scattered. Those that survived made their way home by going round the top of Scotland and the west coast of Ireland."

Edith's mind stirred with the possibilities of the idea Ernie had presented her with. "I presume the purpose was to deter them, not simply to create a cloud of fog. Any skilled captain could navigate his way through oceans of cloud and turbulent seas. It was something far greater than a mere storm those witch ancestors of yours were calling up, wasn't it?"

Ernie said nothing more, but there was a sly smile on his face.

"You must tell me everything you can remember, Ernie dear. Anything, no matter how fragmentary, could hold the vital clues we need to recreate a grand sabbat."

Now the idea had been mooted, it seemed obvious and Edith mentally chided herself for not thinking of it first. The notion took root in her mind and her sense of frustration and helplessness was replaced completely by the excitement and anticipation of hatching a grand plan. A grand ceremony would be just the thing to allay the vast ocean of helplessness she was feeling in these awful, troubled days.

"What can you tell us about the ritual itself? I remember Dad talking about it, years ago." Susie asked her brother. "Do you suppose he kept any records?"

"'Ernie," Edith interrupted, "do tell me that you have something written down! You say this cone of power is a force, an entity raised by the witches. I think I know how that can be done, with dancing and chanting and so forth, but was its purpose to affect the Armada itself or to create the storm that sent them packing? We would need to be very clear about exactly what it is we are trying to achieve and each one of us should have the very same intention to create a powerful force to that specific end. We may need to round up more people to take on such a task."

"And there you have hit the proverbial nail on its head." Ernie said. "Group focus and combined energy is the only possible way to achieve such magic.

Edith grasped hold of Susie's hand and squeezed gently. "You couldn't have given me a more appropriate course of action to take, Ernie. How soon can it be done?"

"Let's not get carried away." Ernie's steely eyes met hers across the table, giving the impression that his mind was busily scheming away. "We shall have to gather our forces first, if we're to succeed."

"Yes, that makes sense." Edith agreed, her quick mind already casting back and forth to assess which of her friends and acquaintances might prove suitable. "People of like mind who can be discrete and sensible about it."

Ernie looked thoughtful for a moment, then his eyebrows raised. "There are several people we might call upon. Kitty could be considered. She is a talented author I'm acquainted with."

"Kitty? Are you referring to Katherine Oldmeadow? I had no idea she was one of us." Susie said.

Ernie nodded, rubbing the tips of his fingers across his chin thoughtfully. "I'm not certain that she is, as you put it, one of us exactly, but she may be quite supportive if nothing else."

"I know her too, as it happens, I shall pay her a visit." Edith replied.

"Well, I will leave it to you to decide who is best suited for our purposes. What are your thoughts, Gerald?"

Gerald, who had been quiet for some time, replied, "I shall give the matter some thought. It's very good of you to include me in your discussions, especially as I am relatively new to the magical arts. I am not sure how much help I could be myself, though I can certainly ask some of my acquaintances if they would like to be involved."

"That's all very well, Gerald," Edith began, "but I do hope you will keep it on the hush-hush."

"Please don't worry yourself," he tapped his nose, "I shall be cautious."

"You had better be," she warned him, "we cannot risk rumours of witchcraft spilling out all over the place."

~ SIXTEEN ~

Tea and Tears

Wednesday 22nd May 1940

A cold swell of wind buzzed suddenly, sweeping up leaves and twigs in a swirling cascade of rustling and rushing, and doing nothing whatever to help matters. A large wicker trug basket over one arm, Edith picked out the secateurs and snipped off the dead heads of several pastel pink roses that had blossomed and faded, their fragrance all but gone and the delicate petals wilted and beginning to dry. The bare stems looked forlorn and barren, but the plant would soon start sending its energy up to the remaining blooms and the colours would stand out once more. She had always been fond of roses and there were several of her favourite varieties in her garden. Pink, red, yellow, orange, white, cream and variegated; dusky, bright, pale or vivid. The display the rose bushes put on for her each year was one of life's simple pleasures as far as she was concerned and served to take her mind off the day's newspaper reports.

The British Expeditionary Force, stationed in France, were on the verge of being pushed back to Dunkirk and every day, every hour, the nation listened to the wireless for news of loved ones. Women mourned for their husbands, lovers and sons. Youngsters grieved for their fathers, their brothers and their peers and there was precious little comfort to be had for any of them. How could these soldiers, called up to duty without notice and surely with very little in the way of military training, stand a chance against the relentless roar of battle? It didn't matter that lads so young they were barely out of short trousers and school classrooms were in amongst the troops - Hitler took pity on no one.

Edith wondered what the fates would have had in store for her if she had had a son instead of a daughter. She only hoped that Ernie was right and the witches could pull off this cone of power.

Distracted by such thoughts, she caught her arm on a rose thorn and gave out a small, sharp noise of pain. She dropped the rose she was holding and rubbed the spot where a pinprick bead of dark red began to form, and then another distraction caught her attention.

"Yoo-hoo, hello Edith!" Said a disembodied voice. "Everything all right over there?"

"Just caught my arm on a rose thorn." She replied, hoping she kept the testiness out of her voice as Ruth from next door popped her head over the fence that separated their rear gardens.

"Always with the roses, eh? Don't know where you find the time, darling."

"Oh, you know me," Edith said. "I like to keep busy." Unlike Ruth who, in Edith's opinion, had far too much time on her hands and was quite the opposite of busy.

"They are looking a little run-down though, what with the time I have to spend on the vegetables I've planted. Over there, see?" She pointed out the patch of growing produce, but her neighbour merely sighed and began her idle chattering once more.

The woman was nice enough, she supposed, even if she seemed to do little else but sunbathe in her garden with a book in one hand and a large glass of red wine or a G-and-T in the other.

Edith managed to trim a few more dead heads and tidy up a stray branch or two while Ruth regaled her with the mundane details of her life. She had a pleasant-sounding voice and it helped the time pass, but she did so wish the woman would stop droning on about her sister so much. And better that Edith didn't even think about Ruth's awful nephew. Ruth's interest in her sister's eldest child was overbearing; any mothering instincts the woman had were thrust upon the lad with gusto. Edith almost felt sorry for him, unbearable though he was. On the few occasions she'd seen him on rare visits to his aunt and uncle, she'd seen him do nothing but scratch his name into tree bark, kick balls around noisily, and swear almost incessantly. Charlie's school days had not been productive ones for the young man, and he had found himself a Saturday job at the butchery until he turned seventeen in September, when he promptly joined the army and was sent off to fight shortly after. Seventeen was no age to be fighting in a war, no matter how disruptive or annoying the lad might be.

Edith was of half a mind to tell Ruth exactly what she thought of darling Charlie. No, those kinds of thoughts were best left unsaid. The poor woman was simply lonely, with her husband busy at work for long periods and no children of her own to care for.

She realised the babbling stream of words had been replaced with soft sobs and sniffles.

She put down her secateurs and took off her gardening gloves, laying them on her little potting table, and went across to the fence where Ruth was crying over her glass of whatever tipple it held today. Ruth's face was wet with tears and her free hand wiped at the mess of damp mascara under her eyes. The result made her look like a sad panda and Edith couldn't help feeling a rush of sympathy for the woman. Edith valued her privacy and didn't really want to invite Ruth into her home, where her inquisitive nose might sniff out anything out of the ordinary. Still, those misty eyes and the damp handkerchief that Ruth now shoved against her face, cried out for someone to listen. It was unbearable, really.

"You'd better come inside." Edith reached over the fence and patted Ruth on the shoulder. "Come around to the door, Ruth. I shall put the kettle on to boil and you can tell me all about it."

Whatever the cause of her neighbour's tears, and Edith suspected it was Ruth's over-active imagination causing worry when there was no need for it, what mattered was that a woman in need had a friendly neighbour to rely on when she needed one. Providing a little comfort and solace was the right thing to do.

Settled in the cosy kitchen, Edith put two plain biscuits onto a china plate, neatly placed in the centre of a lace doily along with teapot, cups, saucers and a small jug of milk. Her favourite teapot was decorated with delicate pink and yellow roses and the crockery was just as pretty, though she lamented the loss of the matching milk jug which had broken years ago and which she had since replaced with a plain white one.

"No sugar I'm afraid," Edith poured a little milk into each cup before stirring the tea, "and the tea isn't as strong as I would normally take it, but you know how things are these days."

"I'm sure it will do nicely." Ruth gave a hint of a smile and the two women shared a sad glance. "Ration coupons are all very well and good but when the shops have run out, what use are they?"

"I queued for nearly an hour at the grocery yesterday and when I was second-in-line, Mr Fletcher came out and announced he'd run out of ham, bacon and eggs! All that time standing in the rain for nothing. Never mind, we have to make the most with what we do have, don't we? Now, let's have a biscuit and you can tell me what's on your mind."

"It's Charlie." Ruth blew on her tea before taking a small, noisy sip. Edith resisted the urge to tut loudly and nodded instead in what she hoped was a sympathetic expression.

"I believe you've mentioned him once or twice. How is he faring?"

"We don't know. That's the trouble." Ruth went on, again making a small noise as the tea went down. "Our Jenny hasn't heard from him. He sent a letter every month, regular as clockwork. Two of them in February, but nothing since then." The tears started up again and Edith moved her chair closer to give a consoling hug until the sobs subsided. Charlie might be an erstwhile trouble maker but like hundreds, thousands, of other young men called to arms, he was little more than a boy, younger than Rosanne, and she could imagine all too well the heart-break and worry his lack of communication must be causing.

"I expect his letters have been lost, that's all. It's not necessarily bad news." But they both knew that yes, the sudden absence of regular communication most likely did mean that bad news was on the way, and probably sooner rather than later.

"Jenny's hardly left the house the last few weeks in case the phone rings. Do they telephone, do you think? With news like that?" Ruth wondered aloud. "Or maybe it'll be a telegram."

"I'm afraid I couldn't say." The look in Ruth's eye, a watery gaze full of false hope overlaid with fear, made her worry for the poor woman.

It also made her determined to do whatever she could to keep Britain safe. Playing her part in the ARP patrolling the night-time streets was important and now, as she continued to make sympathetic small talk with Ruth, her mind was busy making plans for another role for her to play; that of a Priestess organising a grand sabbat.

~ SEVENTEEN ~

Keep Our Soldiers Safe!

Wednesday 22nd May 1940

Evening

A spring time breeze hung in the air fresh with the aroma of petrichor, that peculiar smell one only ever noticed in damp woodlands, that lingered after the heavy rain had fallen in such a hurry earlier in the day, leaving everything in the forest rich with the promise of growth and nourishment. The earthen path beneath her feet was solid and wholesome, if still a little damp, and Edith was sorely tempted to take off her shoes and stockings so that she could roam off the path and enjoy the tickling of grass between her toes. Had she been alone, she would have done just that but alas, she was not. Although, she reflected, her companions were not likely to raise too strong an objection if she did bare her feet and might even join her in the childish act. Time, however, was not on their side and she quickened her step. The more she dilly-dallied, the longer it would take and though not a cold evening, the breeze was picking up somewhat and blustering through the whispering leaves on the trees and bushes all around.

"Thank you both again for coming out on such short notice, I wouldn't normally call on you but poor Ruth was so upset and I simply have to do something."

"Of course. Are we nearly there yet?" Susie Mason piped up, bringing up the rear of the little group that trudged in Edith's wake.

"Always impatient, dear sister," Ernie teased.

"Will you please be quiet? This is a serious matter and I am sure I did ask you to remain focused at all times."

"We are taking it seriously, aren't we, Susie?"

"Of course," Susie replied, "and I'm sure it's not much farther, is it?"

Edith stopped in her tracks and turned to face her fellow conspirators and witches. "I can see your brain working, Susie, trying to decide if I've lost my bearings and I can assure you, I have not. We've arrived."

Edith pointed to the left, away from the narrow path they'd been following through the trees, where a hawthorn, in full bloom with its delicate, creamy white flowers full of promise, hung low between two gnarly oaks to create a kind of doorway or lintel. She ducked underneath the hawthorn boughs, signalling behind for the other two to follow. The thick stand of trees and undergrowth opened to reveal a nicely hidden gem of a ritual spot. Perfectly invisible from the path unless you were looking right at it.

Edith held a spiked branch out of the way to let Ernie and Susie climb underneath. As brother and sister took a moment to become familiar with the location she'd picked out for this evening's ritual, Edith wasted no time in taking the tools of her craft out of the wicker basket she'd been carrying. A wooden wand, silver chalice, red wine, offering bowls, candles with glass jars to stand them in, and a thick, black, woollen cloak that she was pleased she'd remembered to bring. The breeze was picking up and she would be glad of the extra warmth it provided later, when the night's darkness stole away the sun's warmth.

A quietness descended upon the trio and the dusk had drawn close and still. Standing in silence, gathering in the grounding energy of earth beneath and the sky above, looking into each other's eyes to make a connection. A few minutes more, then Edith nodded. They were ready.

From a deep pocket hidden in the folds of her cloak, she pulled a newspaper clipping from today's paper which included two photographs of local young men, soldiers who had been commended for their bravery in combat. Edith had thought better of asking Ruth for a photograph of Charlie so this would have to suffice. She placed it carefully on a small plate in the centre of the circle, a pebble on top to hold it there. Ernie and Edith, as Priest and Priestess, called to the four directions and cast the circle while Susie clapped her hands, slow and tuneless, adding her energies to the magical boundary. Edith spoke to the ancestors, the old protectors of the land, asking for their help to watch out over the British troops deployed overseas. Her words were echoed by Susie and Ernie and the three of them joined hands and began to call out words of protection, pleading for the safe return of her neighbour's nephew, among dozens of others.

Slowly they started to circle deosil, chanting and calling out, and soon they went faster, feet flying over the grass, cloaks fluttering, pulses racing. The wind carried their voices away and the rustling trees added their whispering voices to the mix. Every fibre of her being was bristling with energy and, if she squinted in just the right way, Edith could half-see the swirling vortex of power that played in the air around them in a dance of silver and white light. Her whole body felt charged with electricity and confirmed that raising a cone of power would very likely be every bit as successful as Ernie had mooted. The thought of it thrilled her.

"Circle of protection, hear our plea, let all those at war be kept safe, keep our soldiers safe." They kept it up until everyone could feel the power between them growing in strength and then, with a war-like cry, Edith shouted out, "Release!"

Coming to a sudden halt, the three witches thrust their arms up, hands reaching to the heavens to release the energy and they breathed hard and fast.

"So it will be." said Edith, repeated by Ernie and Susie. Nothing more needed to be said. The magic was done and all that remained now was to give thanks to the powers they called into the circle. This was done by sharing sloe gin, passed between them with a chaste kiss, and another portion poured onto the earth. An offering, a token of gratitude and thanks to the earth that had created this place of deep green, of wood and stone, of leaf and flower, of deer and fox and all things sacred to the heart of a witch.

Packing away the ritual tools and glass candle jars back into her basket, Edith shook leaves out of her hair and patted it back into place. There were scuffs of mud on her otherwise shiny shoes and those would need a jolly good polish when she got home but she had always loved the outdoors and that was all part of the experience. Part of her life really, she mused.

"I can't thank you both enough for adding your energies to this spell. Ruth doesn't know, of course, but I do hope that it will help her nephew. I must add that I would not ordinarily perform any spells without the person's permission. This was, however, personal to me, my ears need a rest from Ruth's worrisome talk. However, I may have to bring my wellingtons next time."

"Next time?" Asked Susie. "What more can we do?"

Edith hadn't realised she had been thinking aloud. "This war shows no signs of coming to an end. The ritual we've just done was just the tip of the iceberg. You felt the energy we raised tonight, didn't you?"

"Of course," said Susie, her brother nodded in agreement. "It was quite significant, I felt."

Edith grinned, her eyes wide, and she nodded her head. "Precisely. Think how much better it would be with even more occultists at a Grand Sabbat, as your brother suggested. I will go ahead discuss it with Katherine Oldmeadow, I have her telephone number."

As the little group walked back towards their bicycles and cycled the short distance back to Edith's bungalow, they discussed the possibilities.

"Might I suggest Rosamund Sabine? She has a lifetime of esoteric knowledge and was once a member of the Golden Dawn."

"You mean Mother Sabine? She must be in her seventies by now. I hardly think she would want to be traipsing through the forest in the middle of the night."

"There are other ways she could help. She has a great many contacts from her time in the Golden Dawn and other societies."

"It has been some time since I paid her a visit, I shall call on her in the next few days. I'll be in her neighbourhood in any case, as I'm going to visit Gerald."

"That's a surprise, Edith." Susie raised her eyebrows and grinned.

Edith scowled at her in mild disapproval. "I'm going to consult some volumes in his library, if you must know. He has a very fine collection of books on magical traditions and the occult."

"Give Gerald our best regards, won't you, darling?"

"I will, and I apologise again that I couldn't offer a place for you to stay this evening." Edith waved cheerily as they parted company and the Masons headed off to catch the train back to Southampton.

There was little room to spare at Theano, certainly not enough for overnight visitors, and not for the first time the idea of moving to a larger property entered her mind. She wasn't sure her finances were up to it and with so many other things to think of, moving to a new house wasn't her first priority.

~ EIGHTEEN ~

Cream Tea

Saturday 25th May 1940

Rosetta and Susie Mason grinned as Edith told them her latest news. Between them was a delicate ornamental plate with roses swirling on its edges, though the scones the plate had once held were now reduced to nothing more than crumbs. The three friends were taking their cream-tea in a quaint and intimate teahouse in Southampton, Edith having taken the train there to meet the sisters. It had been a long week of teaching and she deserved a day off. Besides, it had been a long time since Rosetta, the third of the Mason siblings, had been able to join them as most of her time was taken up with her own young family.

"Ruth was in tears when she told me," Edith explained. "Happy tears, fortunately. Charlie, her nephew, has finally been in touch. In fact, one month's worth of letters turned up all at once. She and her sister had a wonderful time reading them yesterday."

"That is good to hear," Susie agreed, "our little escapade was worth it, then."

"Escapade?" Rosetta asked. "Did I miss something interesting?"

"Nothing too exciting," Edith replied, "my neighbour's young nephew, who signed up some time ago, had not been heard of recently, and Susie and Ernie very kindly helped with a ..."

At this point, Edith turned her head around and surveyed the adjacent tables, making sure that none of the other patrons were paying attention. The only other customers were a party of four, from whose table came raucous laughter every few minutes.

Eyeing up these others, she lowered her voice, to be on the safe side.

"I will only say that we did something about it." She would have resisted the urge to wink furtively, if that manner of expression had been in her nature.

"You do know what she means, sis?" Added Susie, leaning towards her sister with wide eyes.

Rosetta stared at them both blankly and then caught on. "Oh! I see. Well, then that is good news."

"Of course," Edith sighed, "this does mean that I will have to endure the dubious pleasure of listening to Ruth reading some of these letters to me over the garden fence if I'm spotted pruning while she takes her afternoon G-and-T on the sun lounger. Did I mention that she wore nothing but a minuscule two-piece bathing suit on Tuesday? I know it was unseasonably hot that day, but really!"

Susie, who knew full well that Edith herself, against appearances of being prim and proper, was not averse to showing more than a hint of naked skin when the mood took her, hid the smirk on her lips and picked up the colourful teapot. To her disappointment, it produced only a thin, short dribble of liquid.

"May we have another pot please?" She caught the attention of their waitress, who nodded cheerfully and stirred from her place at the counter and shortly produced a fresh pot.

"Sorry, Edie, what were you saying?" Susie helped herself to two brown sugar lumps and stirred them into her tea.

"He should never have been accepted as a soldier to begin with." Edith folded her arms and shook her head.

"Why ever do you say that?" asked Rosetta.

"The boy had only just turned seventeen years old - seventeen - when he donned his military uniform. He's younger than my daughter."

"What of it? There are thousands of soldiers younger than that, as you very well know."

"That's quite true," Susie agreed. "Many young lads are deliberately misleading about their ages, so keen are they to do their bit."

"Young women too, I shouldn't wonder." Rosetta put in.

"I'm thankful that Rosanne hasn't got it into her head to sign up. Several of her acquaintances have done so. One of her friends has taken a position as land-girl, planting, weeding, pulling up crops, that sort of thing, and it's back-breaking work with very little pay. I think if it were not for Rosanne's relationship with Tommy, it might have been different."

"Speaking of whom, how are the plans for their wedding coming along, Edith?"

"There is still a lot to organise and thank goodness there is still time to do it all before the big day. I have been quite distracted," she glanced across to check if the waitress was close enough to overhear, "with other things."

"That reminds me, Edith," said Rosetta, "did you visit with Mother Sabine?"

"She wasn't at home when I called, and my teaching has kept me busy since. I do intend to try again very soon."

"I see. Well, I did have a look through the remaining papers of father's that I remembered, but there wasn't anything useful. I had wondered if there might be any further detail about the Armada and how the ritual was done then."

"Susie told me what you are planning, with your Grand Sabbat. How exciting!"

"Hush," Edith scolded mildly, very aware that they were in danger of drawing attention to themselves if anybody was listening. Fortunately, it seemed that the other patrons were absorbed in their own conversations. Still, a smouldering heat began to bubble under her skin and Edith drew in a deep breath to calm herself, closing her eyes for a moment and dampening the fire inside. She should have expected one or other of the Mason sisters to bring the subject up. After all, their mutual fascination with the occult and all things mystical was a large part of what drew them together as friends, but it was unreasonable, to her mind, that they seemed content to talk of such things in any old time or place.

"Flaunt your own affairs if you must, but I am a respected teacher, and I will not risk my reputation being put into jeopardy with talk of such activities in the open." Edith's voice was barely above a whisper but there was a harsh edge in her tone.

"Oh, darling," Susie leaned over and pressed her hand to Edith's, squeezing it gently, "we didn't mean to upset you."

"I know that was never your intention, but really, Susie, I won't have it!" Edith snatched up her purse from the table and shook her head. "I have come all the way here for a pleasant visit with the two of you to take my mind off all the trouble and worry, not to drag our plans out into the light of day for a public airing."

Rosetta lowered her head and, very wisely, said nothing. Susie, however, pursed her lips and retaliated. "I can't help but think you are overreacting, Edie. Look around," she made a sweeping gesture to illustrate her point, "there are four other persons here, sitting at the other end of the tearoom to us. Our waitress is lounging by the counter with nothing to do but read whatever periodical she has in front of her."

"That is not my point!" Edith, still gripping her purse, struggled to put on her coat and stood up to leave. "Now, if you will excuse me, I have other matters to attend to."

Saturday 1st June 1940

DAILY MAIL

Bloody Marvellous!

For days past thousands upon thousands of our brave men of the B.E.F. have been pouring through a port somewhere in England, battle-worn, but, thank God, safe and cheerful in spite of weariness. We may hope that already at least half of that gallant force has been withdrawn from the trap planned for them by Nazi ruthlessness.

Praise in words is a poor thing for this huge and heroic effort. But praise we must offer for all engaged, and for the brilliant leadership in the field … Praise, then, for him and for them! "A bloody marvellous show", says a high officer.

~ NINETEEN ~

Scouting for Recruits

Tuesday 4th June 1940

Gerald's library was a haven of peace and quiet and after her falling out with Susie and Rosetta, Edith needed that sense of tranquillity. Reading through several volumes on witchcraft, spells and incantations, research for the proposed cone of power the group intended to raise, she made a note of any information they could use to their advantage.

Gerald had spotted straight away that something was bothering her and wasted no time in mentioning that her auric body was dark with what he described as fizzing grey bubbles of uneasiness at the edges. Whether he brought this up because he was concerned about her well-being or if he wanted to show off his skill in the aura reading techniques he'd been practicing was up for debate. Probably a little of both, she mused.

"I'm sure the Mason sisters meant no harm, dear. Might it be the case that your response was a little, shall we say, excessive?"

Her immediate reaction to Gerald's suggestion was one of indignation but she forced herself to pause and reflect on his words. "Perhaps I am being overly sensitive about it. I shall speak to Susie and put things right between us soon, I promise."

"Very good. Now, I know that my books are a wonderful collection and I hope you managed to find what you were looking for, but you have been here more than two hours already and I know you wanted to visit Mother Sabine today."

Edith glanced at the clock on the wall and realised that he was right. "Time has quite run away with me, it seems. I shall see you again soon, Gerald. Goodbye for now."

It was a pleasant walk down Elphinstone Road, across the Common and then to the end of Avenue Road to Rosamund's house, Whinchat. Edith had grown very fond of this part of Highcliffe with its swathes of common land where wildflowers grew in the abundant hedgerows and birdsong trilled out from the trees. Familiar with the route across the common, she was able to spot the call of goldfinch, chaffinch and great tit. There was an old holly, waving the spiky leaves as she rubbed her fingers against as she passed, and here were beech and ash, proud and strong.

Her growing friendship with Gerald was only one of the reasons she thought that Highcliffe would be a positive move and since leaving the Crotona Fellowship, there was nothing to keep her in Somerford. Edith pushed the thought to the back of her mind for now, and turned onto Avenue Road, wondering what kind of reception she might expect from Rosamund. On good terms with each other, it was nevertheless a good six months or more between visits and that was normally to exchange herbal recipes or catch up on general gossip and news. How the elderly woman might react to Edith's enquiries of such an explicit magical nature was anybody's guess.

Whinchat, Rosamund and George Sabine's home, on the corner of Avenue Road and Chewton Farm Road, was a large, impressive detached house set in substantial grounds secluded by a stand of trees.

Edith stepped up to the porch and pulled the old-fashioned bellpull, which was connected to a bell ringing somewhere in the depths of the house. After what seemed like an age, the door was opened by an old woman with white hair and piercing blue eyes. Rosamund Sabine was a striking figure, though not tall, and held herself high. She was dressed neatly in a tweed twinset, not unlike one of Edith's own.

"Edith, what a lovely surprise. To what do I owe the pleasure? You've missed George, I'm afraid. Gone fishing. Come along inside, just mind the jars with herbal preparations on the floor there. I've been busy making the usual concoctions for the usual purposes."

Edith decided not to enquire further. The concoctions were most likely teas and tisanes to stave off colds and treat a range of mild illnesses and disorders and she thought it was also likely that some of those jars had magical purposes.

"Do have a seat, just move the books."

A faint and musty smell, like old paper and moth balls, filled the cluttered house. It was homely and comfortable, however, with assorted jars and bottles of herbs, and books spread open or stacked haphazardly about the place. A wooden table was laid out with several volumes of delicately illustrated books on the medicinal uses of herbs, botany and plant identification.

Edith stacked a couple of books together to free up a straight-backed chair and sat at the table. Rosamund gestured to the cluttered wooden table-top where a teapot was almost hidden amongst the assorted jars of herbs and flowers which were, no doubt, part of her unnamed preparations for the usual things.

"Should still be hot enough for a cup, do help yourself, dear."

Edith declined the offer of tea. "I can't stay for long, I'm afraid, though I promise to call on you again when I have more time."

"I suspected this was not merely a social visit. Why don't you tell me what's on your mind?"

Not sure quite where to begin, Edith came straight out with it.

"It's becoming apparent from recent news reports that the Nazis are not going to be easily defeated and there are numerous threats facing our country right now. The threat that affects us most, living on the coast as we do, is that of the enemy invading from the sea. To that end, we are going to stage a Grand Sabbat, to raise what is described as a cone of power, a vortex of magical energy. Our intention is to halt the German invasion from overseas."

She waited patiently and slightly nervously to hear Rosamund's thoughts on this. Would the older woman be understanding or was she about to hear all the reasons why such an undertaking was ill-advised?

"I had wondered myself if the psychically inclined would be working on the astral plane against the Nazis. You won't be the only ones planning to take action in this way. That, or something similar, I'm sure."

Edith nodded with agreement. "We hope that with enough forceful will-power and dynamic energy hitting them in the face, the axis will crumble and reconsider their plans for a full-scale invasion."

"I think you would need to plan very carefully, dear. The right date, the time of year, the phase of the moon, should all be as conducive to your aims as possible. I would rather like to be involved myself, if you have no objections."

"Oh, that is good to hear, I'm pleased to have your support," Edith smiled warmly, "I must warn you, however, that we will be skyclad and there will be a lot of dancing involved. I wouldn't expect you to join in with every aspect of the ritual, though you would be most welcome to take part in whatever way you see fit when everything is in place."

"Very good." Rosamund picked up a bundle of rosemary from among the plants and books on the table and began to chop it roughly with a small pair of kitchen scissors. "Pass me that big bowl, would you? The blue one behind you."

Edith reached for the bowl and put it beneath Rosamund's busy hands to catch the rosemary. Plenty of it had already fallen to the tabletop and she scooped it up, depositing the fragrant green shards into the bowl, and then brought her hands to her face and inhaled the beautiful scent.

"There was one other thing, if you don't mind. We think it would be helpful and strengthen the ritual if more people were involved. Do you know of anyone who would have sufficient psychic awareness and ability to fit in with what we are planning?"

Rosamund stopped what she was doing, sat back in her chair and closed her eyes. She looked as if she were deep in thought, hands folded neatly in her lap.

At last, as Edith was beginning to think that she was falling asleep, Rosamund opened her eyes and leant forward in her chair. She looked directly at Edith.

"Did you know that when I lived in Sussex, before the last war, I was a member of a coven? We used to meet up on the Downs, in Chanctonbury Ring. It was a long while ago and, unfortunately, I've lost touch with most of the members, other than my friend Helen. Helen will be there like a shot, if I know her! Harry Byngham is made of the right stuff, now that I think of it. I don't know if he's on the phone, but I will try and talk to him. Leave it to me. I'll see what I can do. "

"Thank you, that's very good of you."

"By the way," Rosamund continued, surprising Edith with her sudden return of vigour, "How is your new initiate coming along? Gardner? Do bring him round for tea some time soon."

Edith laughed, flustered for once, and nodded, taking Rosamund's hands in hers. "I am sure you would like him very much. He is - oh, I don't know quite how to describe Gerald."

"You deserve some enjoyment in your relationships after all you've gone through in recent years."

On the short walk back to Southridge on Highland Avenue, Edith reflected on Rosamund's parting words. It was high time she had some enjoyment in her life, or at the very least, a close companion and confidante. She believed she had found just that, in Gerald.

~ TWENTY ~

Who and Where?

Wednesday 5th June 1940

The tension was palpable, every eye in the room either downcast with anxious worry or open wide in anticipation. Nobody dared move or murmur a sound, lest they miss the vital news coming from the radio as the tinny, disembodied voice filled the room, imparting the events of the day.

The majority of troops of the British Expeditionary Force had been rescued from the shores of Dunkirk, the newsreader announced, many of them after several bone-chilling hours of uncertain waiting while waist or shoulder-deep in the sea before boarding the rescue boats. One could only imagine the horror of being trapped on the beaches with advancing enemy forces rushing in from all sides, with only the cold and forbidding sea to retreat to as a means of escape. The stiff, upper-class voice boomed on. Still more soldiers were returning, even as the news continued to come in, relayed as quickly as possible to keep the public notified of the latest progress in this difficult rescue operation.

"Operation Dynamo," Gerald huffed, "we should have an operation code-name of our own, don't you agree?"

"Hush, it's the P.M. now." Ernie put a finger to his lips and leaned closer to the wireless. He fiddled with the tuning dial for the clearest signal and turned up the volume.

> *"Even though large tracts of Europe and many old and famous states have fallen or may fall into the grip of the Gestapo and all the odious apparatus of Nazi rule, we shall not flag or fail.*

> We shall go on to the end. We shall fight in France, we shall fight on the seas and oceans, we shall fight with growing confidence and growing strength in the air, we shall defend our island, whatever the cost may be. We shall fight on the beaches, we shall fight on the landing grounds, we shall fight in the fields and in the streets, we shall fight in the hills; we shall never surrender."

Churchill's speech, even when heard second-hand as a broadcast, was a rousing one. Nobody could deny it, and if a tear or two were shed as they listened, well, nobody could be blamed for that.

"Historic, utterly historic," Gerald said after Edith switched off the radio. "Only a few scant weeks in the position of Prime Minister and look what a rallying war-cry he makes!"

"You're wrong, Gerald," Rosanne said, "to sound so damnably pleased about it. Who cares what the Prime Minister says, when for every one of those soldiers who were rescued, there are probably two more who didn't make it back alive, or if they did, then not in one piece? We may have avoided them at the Dunkirk seaport but how long will it take for the Axis to follow our ships across the channel and strike us down on our own soil?"

"Rosanne, really," Edith placed a hand on her daughter's shoulder but was shrugged off. "You're exaggerating; there were over three-hundred-thousand fellows who returned safely and-"

"It's true, though, isn't it? They *will* come here now." The young woman continued, determined to have her say. "All we can do is wait like fish in a barrel to get picked off one by one! I can't stand it, I tell you!" Tears welled up in her eyes like fat, sad rain drops and spilled onto her cheeks. Rosanne wiped them roughly and ran from the room, leaving them with the sounds of footsteps clattering in the hallway and the slamming of her bedroom door. No good running after her, Edith knew, Rosanne would feel better after some time alone and good night's sleep.

The dreaded rough beast had left its lair, its hour come round at last. If Britain was the proverbial Bethlehem that Yeats had proposed not so very long after the end of the last war, then she was determined to do all that was within her power to stop that slouching beast in its deadly tracks.

"He shall not come." She stood up suddenly, surprising even herself with the forceful, decisive tone of her voice. "We cannot stand by and see this invasion come to our shores. Let me quote a line of Gerald's book to you. Dayonis says: *'cannot a witch have her uses sometimes?'* Well, we do have our uses: we shall hold the greatest ritual the British Isles have seen in over a hundred years. We must act, now. The time has come for us to stop talking and make our arrangements for Operation Cone of Power."

"Agreed! Perhaps before anything is decided, we should find a location for the ritual." Ernie said. "So, what would be the requirements?"

"Well," Edith replied. "It needs to be private, naturally, either indoors or in some place outside sufficiently remote to be away from prying eyes. I should say I strongly favour the latter."

"There are plenty of places in the New Forest where we can be well away from the public gaze, not to mention out of sight of the ARP wardens and the Home Guard."

"It would have to be a large, clear space for a circle, which, if we get as many people as we want, would need to be reasonably big."

"Ernie, you know the New Forest very well, don't you?"

"Yes, we stayed at Bolderwood with the Tames on numerous occasions. We explored that part of the Forest very thoroughly over the years. There are several areas that we could appropriate; Mark Ash Wood and down towards the Knightwood Oak, and then there is the area around the Rufus Stone."

Susie nodded in agreement and jotted down the locations in her notebook. Edith made a point of catching Susie's gaze and smiling. Although the two women were friends once more, their previous disagreement was still on both of their minds and she, at least, was determined to keep things between them on an even keel.

"Thank you, Susie. I shall check my teaching schedule and find some time to visit the locations in person."

"Let's get down to practicalities, shall we?" interjected Ernie. "Who is taking part in the ritual and how are they getting there?"

"Well, there's you and me, Edith and Gerald. That's four. Edith, what did you decide about Rosanne and her young man?"

"She is of the opinion that Tommy would take it seriously so put them down as a possibility. I've paid a visit to Rosamund Sabine and she would like to come with her husband George. Rosamund also mentioned an acquaintance of hers, Harry Byngham, who sounds like a good fit for us, and another lady and her husband. They were in a coven together and Rosamund assures me they will be more than sympathetic to our aims."

"If I might interject," Gerald leaned forward and held a single, wagging finger in the air thoughtfully, "it occurs to me that Walter Forder might be an appropriate candidate for us. He is a most agreeable fellow, and as you know, he has a particular interest in occult matters.'"

"Oh what a splendid idea, Gerald. Do ask him, won't you? Katherine Oldmeadow will have a word with one or two people she thought might be interested as well her sisters and Mr. Lawrie. She mentioned a blacksmith, Charles Loader, who she knows through the gypsies at Thorney Hill. They once told her that he had a lot of magical powers and that he had once been a member of the Horseman's Word."

"What on earth is the Horseman's Word?" Asked Susie.

"A secretive organisation whose members have powers over animals, particularly horses. Apparently they have a secret word to make horses do whatever they wanted them to do."

"Oh, I say, how very curious. Do you suppose this secret word might ..." Gerald leaned forward, keen to hear more, but Ernie cut his words short.

"Focus, Gerald, focus! Now, the locations I believe most suitable are way off the beaten track, and I wouldn't want anyone to get lost on a dark night without any lights showing. I certainly wouldn't want to cycle there, even if it wasn't raining. Although, we could probably avoid that by doing a bit of weather magic. It was quite successful recently, wasn't it, Susie?"

"It was, though we should still choose a place that is easy to reach; not many of us will have vehicles available to get us there. You shall have to fix up our father's old car, Ernie. Rosetta has been asking you to do so for long enough."

She grinned at her brother and batted her eyelids, knowing it would do nothing to sway him but unable to resist it.

"I can't promise anything, but I'll certainly give it a go. Gerald, your friend Walter Forder must have a car, surely? He's always gadding about as part of his job."

Gerald nodded and it was agreed that he and Edith would speak to Walter. After a little more discussion on the who and the where, Edith ushered everyone out of her bungalow and retired for the night. She found herself quietly confident that everything would come together in the end, even if she did have dozens of telephone calls and personal visits to make before then.

~ TWENTY-ONE ~

Gerald Makes An Offer

Thursday 6th June 1940

Late in the evening of the following day, Edith was sitting quietly at her small dining table going through her notes when she heard a very precise pattern of knocking at her door. Not needing to guess who it could be, she called out for her visitor to let himself in.

"Good evening, Gerald. I wasn't expecting you today."

Dressed in long trousers for once, Gerald made himself at home and spread his newspaper open. The Telegraph, in his opinion, was the only periodical worth reading.

"Did you come with some purpose in mind, Gerald, I'm rather busy." She indicated the pile of paperwork she had been poring over, now hidden beneath the newspaper. "I spoke on the telephone today with Mr Lawrie and Kitty Oldmeadow who both confirm they are coming, along with Kitty's sisters. I am meeting with her first thing tomorrow morning and she will introduce me to the blacksmith she mentioned, Charles Loader. I'm very much looking forward to meeting him, sounds a most interesting gentleman. Walter Forder is happy to be involved and, after I pressed him a little, has kindly agreed to pick up one or two others in his car if we need it."

"You must tell me more about this Charles Loader chap, I would be interested in visiting with a blacksmith, I can only imagine the tools he must own. Now, I thought we would visit with Walter together."

"I know, but I was out earlier today and happened to be passing the offices of the Christchurch Times so it made sense to call in and fortunately, he was able to spare me a few minutes to talk things over in his office. Two students came for their lessons this afternoon and since then, I have been going over the Ordnance Survey maps. Perhaps you can take a look, now that you're here. Unless there was some other matter you wished to discuss?"

"There was something yes, but it can wait. Do show me what you mean."

Edith folded Gerald's newspaper out of the way and for the next half an hour they pored over the maps and several rough sketches that Edith had laid on the table: the Naked Man, Mark Ash Wood, Bolderwood.

"It's no good," Edith threw her hands up in despair and quickly shoved all the papers and maps into one large pile, picked them up and placed them out of the way on her already cluttered sideboard. "I simply can't decide on a location by looking at maps and descriptions. I shall have to spend a day traipsing about from one place to the next and I don't have time for that - there is far too much to do and I ..."

"Then allow me to organise the outing. I shall bring us a packed lunch, make sure both our bicycles are in good order and plan a route that takes in all the most likely spots. All you have to do is be ready for a leisurely day out with a good friend to take in the scenery."

"That would actually be quite helpful. Though leave it a week or so, won't you? I have a lot of teaching at the moment."

"I will. Now, there was something else I wished to discuss with you." He did not say anything else immediately, however. Instead, he reached towards her, leaning closely and taking one of her hands into his own. His grip was firm and warm. They faced one another, eyes meeting and locking in, her heart seemed to beat a little faster.

"You told me a short while ago that you are not entirely happy here, Edith, and would like to move away."

"Yes, I remember," she replied, "Ever since I broke my ties with the Crotona Fellowship, there has been nothing to keep me in Somerford. I should like to move to Highcliffe if I could afford to."

"I know, and I have come up with a way in which I can help."

"Gerald, you can't possibly..."

"Please, wait until I have finished before you say anything further." He waited for a moment until he had her focused attention once more. "You would like to relocate, Rosanne and Tommy will need a home of their own when they tie the knot, and I think I have the perfect solution."

Edith removed her hand from his grip and got up to organise a fresh pot of tea. She may need something stronger if Gerald didn't spit it out soon.

"Carry on, dear, I am listening."

"A rather nice property in Highcliffe has come up for sale. I think it would be very suitable for you and it's just along from Rosamund and George Sabine's home on Avenue Road. I can loan you the money for it and you can move there and the newly-weds can take over Theano and rent it from you."

"You've thought this all through, haven't you? I do appreciate your generous offer, really, I do, but I can't possibly see how I can afford to pay you back, not on my teaching salary."

"I have thought of that too. Avenue Cottage is a charming place with a garden and the current owner is selling it and the adjacent house, which is already occupied by paying tenants. If I lend you the money to buy both properties, you would have a regular rental income from the other house, in addition to that which you would receive from Rosanne and Tommy, once they settle in here, at Theano."

Gerald was gently insistent that it would not be any hardship for him to lend her the money and she agreed that Avenue Road was a good location for her to consider.

"After all," she said, "I do have an acquaintance I am rather fond of who lives very close to Avenue Road."

"Is that so?" His merry eyes twinkled, and Edith couldn't supress a little blush as she met his gaze. "Then I shall arrange for us to visit the house at the earliest opportunity. I think you will like it very much."

~ TWENTY-TWO ~

Day Trippers

Saturday 15th June 1940

Gerald rose at half past six, a little earlier than he preferred most mornings, but he had a long day of cycling and exploring ahead of him and needed to set off sharply. The previous evening, he had prepared a basket of sandwiches, scones and apples, and to this he now added two flasks, one of hot tea and one of cold water, and put these into the wicker basket and fastened it by the leather straps to the front of his cycle.

Gerald prepared a breakfast of tea and toast and honey before checking the basket again. Maps, provisions, notebook and pencil. Camera! Where was his blasted camera? Southridge was a pleasant house but with the assorted collections he had gathered and his habit of being rather untidy, it was another ten minutes before he found the camera. Everything in hand, Gerald mounted his bicycle and off he went.

He set a leisurely pace and the going was easy, with only a few inclines to contend with and before long, he arrived at his first port of call. Edith was ready and waiting for him, bicycle propped in front of the low wall outside her bungalow. He was a little surprised to see her wearing a pair of slacks, but he had to admit to himself she did look quite the part of a gentlewoman explorer, and trousers were certainly more practical than the skirts she ordinarily wore. She also had on a wide brimmed hat, secured to her head with a fetching gold and orange scarf. He also noted that her bicycle basket was filled with what looked suspiciously like a feast of a picnic tucked beneath a linen cloth.

He grumbled slightly at this and reminded her that it was he who was organising this trip.

"Very well, I can put the sandwiches and tarts back in the kitchen if you prefer."

At this, Gerald shrugged and acknowledged that if tarts were in the offing, then they may well be hungry enough for two picnics.

"Take this, would you?" He passed her a few sheets of loose paper onto which he had carefully written down the route and directions for her to follow, along with several places of particular interest. "You will notice I have marked down a meeting point or two, in case we find ourselves separated for any reason and there is - Edith? You see, as Churchill himself has declared the Battle of Britain is about to begin, it is imperative that we - are you paying attention?"

"No, I am not." She mounted her bicycle and pushed off, calling out behind her with a lightness to her voice he hadn't hear for some time. "No talk of war or invasion, if you please. You promised I would not need to worry about anything today, so please, can we just enjoy a simple day trip?"

Resigning himself to her stubborn mood, Gerald hopped onto his cycle and set off along the road behind her.

Soon, they had left behind the residential areas of Christchurch and turned onto wide country roads where farmers could be seen hard at work in the crop fields.

A little further on, they skirted Hinton Admiral, and here, his planned route veered away from the main road, taking a smaller, little used track that ran alongside the forest edge. Before long, he noticed to the left and not very far from the long stretch of road, the thick trees of the New Forest opened up to reveal a rough area of grass land where several of the New Forest ponies were busy grazing. The rich, dark chestnut colour of their coats, pure bronze in the dappled sunlight, making the creatures stand out amid wild grasses, majestic and regal. Gerald brought his bicycle to a halt and took out his camera to take a photograph. Standing by a low, wooden fence, he admired the animals for a short time before mounting once again and cycling quickly to catch up with Edith, who by now must be some distance ahead.

Or was she? After another mile or so, there was no sign of her and Gerald wondered if he had taken a wrong turn somewhere along the way. He had thought ahead to the possibility of being separated from one another on their outing and had pointed out to Edith several locations along the intended route as meeting points, should they need them. It would not be long before Gerald reached the first of these so he was not unduly concerned and settled back into the simple enjoyment of the ride.

On he went, through patches of open heath alternating with shrubs and pockets of trees, across a little brook and up a sloping ridge, back onto even ground. Nearing a fork in the road, Gerald decided to venture away from the route he had planned with Edith, thinking that she was surely much farther ahead than he was by now and it would make sense for him to take a more direct road, passing straight through Holmsley on his way towards Burley, a little farther on, which was the first of their agreed-upon meeting points. The weather was fine and the scenery brought him a sense of satisfaction and comfort; everything seemed right with the world, for once, out here in the open with no sight or sound of the war with its myriad of worries and danger. A hundred shades of green, bright yellow of gorse, copper shining ponies, buzzards overhead.

At Burley, he found Edith waiting patiently for him. She was sitting on a low bank of grass at the side of the road, her cycle propped up nearby. She smiled eagerly as he approached and waved at him to stop but he couldn't resist cheekily ringing his bell and speeding off ahead of her. A short giggle of laughter reached his ears and soon they were together again, cycling easily to climb the gentle incline out of the village and into the inclosures of the forest.

Knightwood Inclosure and the Knightwood Oak itself was the first location of specific interest in Gerald's itinerary. Edith dismounted her bicycle here and greeted the Queen of the Forest like a long-forgotten old friend. Approximately five-hundred years old, the Queen was a pedunculate oak of staggering girth, a much-loved and once heavily pollarded tree. Being less than half a day's cycle ride from Christchurch, Gerald knew Edith was as familiar with the oak and its surrounds as he was himself and after a brief time, they continued onward, soon arriving at Mark Ash Wood.

Having now cycled for nearly two hours, Gerald decided it was time to stop for a spot of early elevenses. Propping his bicycle against a friendly looking oak tree, he proceeded to unpack his lunch, took out a tartan picnic rug for them both to sit on. A few minutes later, Edith caught up with him and added her own picnic offerings to share and Gerald happily tucked into the freshly baked goods she laid out. A family of four with an energetic dog walked along the pathway, passing their lunch spot. They exchanged polite greetings while the dog sniffed around to check any food had been left for him.

"Sorry boy, we've eaten it all."

Apart from one other fellow walking a dog earlier in the morning, these were the first people the pair had seen since leaving Burley and Gerald remarked that it was a good indication they were in the right sort of area for midnight rambles. It was certainly far enough away from civilisation that any light from a small fire would not be seen. Edith was inclined to agree.

Mark Ash Wood, depending on the time of year, was an array of colour - purple heather, the bright yellow of gorse in spring and bright golden beech trees turning darker in the autumn. The sharp tangy musk of a fox hung in the air and the tree tops formed an assault course for playful squirrels. There were deer in the Forest too, both fallow and red, though he had seen no sign of them so far. Even an occasional white stag had been spotted in various areas of the New Forest by some lucky folk, though he had never seen one himself. Gerald felt quite at peace here and set off on his own to explore for a time, enjoying the crunch of the forest floor beneath his feet. Here was the magnificent Queen Beech, a gargantuan tree that showed signs of being heavily pollarded in its past. He paid his respects to the long-lived giant with a nod of his head before re-joining Edith and packing up their belongings.

They cycled across heathland, over ridges, across small streams, into gently sloping open spaces and through avenues of trees, exploring the rough tracks of the Forest in search of that perfect spot; somewhere hidden, off the beaten track, a clearing in the trees large enough for their purposes, yet easy to find in the dark if you knew where to look. Even on a warm day such as this, there was barely another soul to be seen. Unless you counted the animals and birds, Gerald supposed; after all, they had souls too. Adders, pipistrelle bats, badgers, wild rabbits, green woodpeckers, tree-creepers and butterflies, they all lived here, along with the deer, foxes and the New Forest ponies. From Mark Ash Wood they travelled through Bolderwood, past Minstead to visit the Rufus Stone and surrounding inclosures, then bypassing Lyndhurst and Brockenhurst before coming to rest for a late afternoon lunch at the weathered and battered tree known locally as the Naked Man in the Wilverley Inclosure area.

The Naked Man, the traditional meeting point of witches hereabouts, was an old and twisted tree with its best years well in the past, a dark and gnarled oak with sharp splits and grooves, most of its bark worn away. Years back, Ernie had once told him, the tree had two prominent branches reaching up, resembling a pair of out-stretched arms which gave rise to the unusual name. Sitting close by the old tree he called to mind another story Ernie had mentioned, something he'd heard from his father and grandfather of the smugglers and highwaymen who had been caught and executed on the gibbet that used to exist at this very location. Gerald shuddered at the thought as he polished off the last of Edith's marmalade tarts.

He began to walk, ambling here and there, while Edith stretched out on the tartan picnic rug, soaking up the warmth of the sun. Looking up at the sky, she'd be lucky if the sun lasted much longer, for the blue sky had the look of summer rain about it now. The high-pitched whispering of crickets in the long grasses brought his attention back to the ground just in time to catch a glimpse of some small, brown creature, tail disappearing beneath grassy green fronds. Mouse. He idly wondered if there were adders about and laughed at himself when he heard himself warning the hapless rodent to proceed with caution.

The Forest held secrets, he knew, if you took the time to look for them. And this, he thought, now reaching a wide expanse of open ground encircled almost completely by trees and thick shrubs, might be one of its best kept secrets. He smiled and took in the clearing more thoroughly. Brush-wood could be used to mark out the boundary of the magic circle and though it was a fair distance from the nearest road, it was certainly large enough for their intended purpose. There was even a low, wide tree-stump - perfect for anyone to perch upon if they were tired, for he was certain the ritual Edith planned would make that likely.

"I say, Edith!" He called out to catch her attention. "Did you take note of this? Just here, a little altar perhaps, or a seat." Eagerly, he pointed it out and trotted around the rough clearing to demonstrate its suitability. She rose and ran over to join him.

"This may very well do, Gerald, well done!" She planted a kiss on his cheek and grabbed his hands, jumping up and down with enthusiasm. Her light-hearted mood was infectious and they whirled madly, round and round until Edith lost her footing. He pulled her arms to stop her from falling and found her face only inches from his, her warm breath on his cheek.

"Gerald, I have had the most tiring week, with one student or another preparing for a test and Rosanne's wedding plans to think of. This has been a perfect distraction. Thank you." Her chin tilted upwards, soft brown eyes twinkling.

Gerald put his arms around her and hugged her close, comforted by the warm, wonderful, magical feel of her in his embrace. And without warning, cold, fat rain began to pelt them and Edith broke away with a squeal.

"Beastly, wretched weather!" She cried out indignantly and dashed back to the Naked Man, where their picnic, blankets and bicycles were now thoroughly drenched. With a heavy heart, Gerald traipsed after her, his thoughts in a whirl.

~ TWENTY-THREE ~

Edith Gets Busy

Sunday 23rd June 1940

"I would rather like to be involved in your event, Edith." Dorothy Fordham's voice crackled over the telephone lines and Edith struggled to catch what she said next.

"Katherine's brother-in-law, Arthur Lawrie, may not be able to join her, I said, so I shall be driving there myself and collecting Kit on my way."

Edith almost regretted asking Katherine Oldmeadow to mention their plans for Operation Cone of Power to Dorothy purely for reasons of safety while transporting everyone to the chosen site. Dorothy Fordham was not the most sensible, reliable or cautious of drivers and so it was with some hesitancy that she agreed to the older woman's suggestion. Fortunately, Edith also knew that Dorothy was not only sympathetic to the subtle energies of magic but also had a keen belief in nature spirits, fairies and their ilk. The addition of such a person to the ritual would be welcome.

"That's very kind of you, Dorothy." Edith said at last, putting to the back of her mind reports of Dorothy's involvement in an accident some years ago. If the thought of driving in the pitch black countryside with only slits for headlights in the middle of the night was not enough to put her off, then nothing would, and Edith would be pleased to have her presence on the night.

Next on her agenda for the day was a visit with Gerald to Avenue Cottage in Highcliffe. A visit she was very much looking forward to. Avenue Cottage turned out to be an ideal home for Edith. Walking through its rooms with Gerald, she felt that she could be quite happy here. Larger than her current home at Somerford, there was more living space than she would require and on seeing the large bay-windowed room to the front of the house, she knew at once that it would be a good-sized-space, letting in lots of light, for her elocution classes. Yes, this place would do very nicely, she thought, and it had the added advantage of being very close in location to several of the best friends she'd ever come to know.

She had intended only to have a quick look at the house, as she was teaching later in the afternoon and needed to prepare, but walking around the rooms, she couldn't help but take time to visualise how her furniture and belongings might look here. A little table just here, a vase of roses in the kitchen window and it would be lovely to sit at her dressing table in the upstairs bedroom, overlooking the rear garden.

Gerald had been waiting patiently for her to tour at her own pace through the empty property after he had shown her the main rooms. When at last she returned to him in the front garden, he offered his elbow to her.

They walked away from the cottage and she glanced back for another look, the corners of her mouth lifting in excitement. She talked rapidly of how she would put this or that room to use and enthused to Gerald that the rear garden was large enough for an abundance of rose bushes.

"My former employer in Baildon had an extensive collection of roses, one of which was named after him. The George C. Waud rose, a very nicely scented tea-rose with delicate yet robust petals of a bright orange-red shade. It would look quite fetching here, along with my other roses"

"I take it by your enthusiastic planning of the garden," Gerald patted the arm she had linked through his as they walked, "that you have decided to take up my offer?"

"If you really mean it, I rather think I shall do just that, and I can't possibly thank you enough."

"It will be thanks enough to see you happy."

"It's terribly kind of you, Gerald." She stopped abruptly and tugged him back from the corner of the road. "I say, would you like to pay a visit with me to Rosamund Sabine? Her home is only a few minutes away and I'm sure she would be very pleased to meet you."

"I did have plans, but as you seem intent on it, we may as well."

Rosamund welcomed them warmly and was soon carrying on a conversation with Gerald that threatened to be overly long, both of them having a habit of talking at length, either about themselves or on the matter of some esoterica or ancient legends. Edith listened for a time, content to let the soft, though animated, discussion wash over her, but eventually, she reminded them that Gerald had plans and she herself did not have all day to listen to idle chit-chat.

"Rosamund, if I may, I'd like to run a suggestion past you."

Rosamund gave a heavy sigh and patted Gerald's hand lightly. "You must visit again, on your own. George would be very keen to meet you."

Edith blinked in astonishment. Not only was Gerald clearly the guest of honour here, but she was almost sure he had just winked at Rosamund! "I am planning our big ritual for the evening of Friday 2nd of August. I wondered if you had any thoughts on the matter and if you can confirm that you will be able to participate?"

"Lammas, eh? A very fitting date," Rosamund turned to glance around her cosy sitting room, spied what she was looking for and took it down from a shelf, holding the object out for Edith to take. "This was last year's corn dolly, perhaps you can burn that on the ritual fire as a sacrifice."

"Thank you," Edith tucked the corn dolly into her handbag, "and you will be there, won't you?"

"Yes, George will be there too. You will let me know when and where to meet, won't you?"

"Yes, several of us are meeting to finalise everything soon. Now, we won't take up any more of your time. Thank you for the tea cakes, by the way."

"Always a pleasure to see you. Mister Gardner, it has been wonderful to meet you." As Rosamund escorted the visitors to the door she held back a moment to whisper in Edith's ear. "He's an absolute delight, this fellow of yours, do bring him again."

That evening, Edith patrolled the streets of Christchurch in her uniform and helmet, on the lookout for illegal lights of the houses she passed. She walked along the coastal path before returning home at the end of her shift, listening to the crunching and rumbling pebbles of the stony beach. She looked out to sea and shuddered with the knowledge that German planes on the distant shores were even now preparing for onslaught; the mighty Messerschmitts, readying to take on the RAF's Spitfires. It was not the cold sea-air that gave her goose pimples, but fear.

~ TWENTY-FOUR ~

How to Influence Hitler

Friday 19th July 1940

"So, we're all agreed that we should include some sort of spell, a form of words which we can repeat, to focus our minds on a single objective. Has anyone ideas for the possible wording of such a spell?"

Gerald spoke up first. "Why don't we just tell him to bugger off?"

"Gerald!" Edith looked at him in disapproval. "I will not have such language in my house! Even if I might agree with the sentiments. We must conduct ourselves in a civilised way, no matter that we are trying to stop someone who is intent on behaving in a most uncivilised way indeed."

Everyone remained quiet for a while, deep in thought. Ernie was the one who broke the silence. "The chief thing is to be clear in our own minds what we want to achieve."

"I thought that was obvious: to stop any threatened invasion."

"All right, but who or what would the spell be directed towards? Would it be Hitler himself or the German High Command? Or would we try some weather magic, as we believe was done on some previous occasions?"

"I think the most obvious thing would be to influence Hitler himself. His word goes, after all, I imagine." Edith kicked off her shoes and tucked her feet up on her chair.

"So, what precisely do we want to change in Hitler's mind?"

"Well, presumably we want to change his mind about the desire to invade this country."

"We don't know that he necessarily wants to invade."

"Of course we do! They've photographed the landing barges along the French coast, we know they are preparing planes and bombs. Everything is building up to an invasion being imminent."

"What about 'you are not able to invade this country?' It's succinct and to the point." Gerald offered.

"No, we want something shorter, punchier, words that virtually say themselves and can be repeated easily. I know your experiences in the coven have been limited so far, Gerald, but we shall not manage long phrases once we are out of breath with dancing to raise the power. Any other suggestions?"

"Not able to cross the sea?"

"Not able to come'?"

"I was thinking of 'Can't cross the sea'."

"Let's combine them." Edith agreed. "We shall chant, 'Not able to come' and 'Can't cross the sea'. Is everybody happy with that?"

Susie once more brought out her notebook and jotted down the chosen phrases.

"Did the two of you find a suitable location?" Asked Ernie. "Somewhere large enough, as I imagine that there will be over a dozen people: the Sabines plus Katherine Oldmeadow, Charles Loader, Walter Forder."

"Yes, Gerald pointed out several parts of the forest I was unfamiliar with and one spot in particular where there are some mature Scots pines in a sort of rough circle. The space within them would definitely be big enough for our purposes."

Gerald nodded and reached into his satchel on the floor to pull out a map. The two men spent several minutes going over the route that had led Edith and Gerald to the most likely site for their ritual.

"I think we all know," Ernie passed the map back to Gerald, "that what we are intending to do is both serious and urgent. For all we know, an invasion might take place tonight. Think for a moment of those young men piloting Hurricanes and Spitfires to protect our land from the enemy. There have been a lot of casualties already, more than have been generally reported, I suspect. Those young men were prepared to sacrifice themselves to defend our country and our people. We must do the same!"

Another long pause, while the implications of that statement sank in to the little group.

"Do you mean that our ritual would involve human sacrifice? I think that would be taking things too far!" Susie said, unhappy with the thought of it.

"No, of course not, but to achieve the result we want, we must be prepared to do something which traditionally was only done in an emergency. The intensity of the working we propose is something which we must put our own life-force into. And that will deplete us, in some cases very seriously. If we are not in the best of health, then the thought-form we have created will seek out your weak spots, rather like the roots of a plant seeking nutrition from the soil. We must be prepared for that eventuality. It will weaken us all, some, of course, more than others. Performing this ritual could be life-changing."

"So, what do we actually need to do? Do we want to cast a circle, for example, or would that inhibit the sending forth of the cone of power?" Edith wondered out loud.

"The circle is partly for protection." Ernie answered, "it will keep us safe from any hostile force that might otherwise become aware of us on the astral plane once we start to raise power. But it will also contain that power and allow us to build it up without it leaking out into the surrounding landscape, until the cone of power has built up sufficiently to be released and sent forth in the direction of our objective."

"Presumably we start to build up power in the usual way, by dancing in a circle?"

"Yes. We can mark the boundary with brushwood and build the circle in the usual way and then raise power by dancing, rushing forwards and chanting the entire time."

"Ernie, I'm trying to remember something that Dad mentioned years ago." Susie squeezed her eyes shut until the memory came to her. "There were two things. One was that they continued circling until someone fainted. They were considered to have taken the spell to its destination."

"That's a bit extreme, isn't it?" said Edith. "It could be very serious for some people. Quite a lot of us are hardly in the first flush of youth."

Ernie answered immediately: "Remember it's the effort that is put into the ritual that is reflected in its successful conclusion. And, as you've said yourself, others are willingly putting their lives in danger to defend their country. What is a little discomfort on our part compared to that?"

"Something else that I think I remember Dad saying was that at some point in the ritual they all linked hands and rushed across the circle in defiance of Boney's intentions to invade."

"Yes, I reckon that at some point the participants would create a straight line across the circle, linking hands."

Edith "That's all very well, but some of us are not in a position to 'rush' anywhere, not at our age!"

"I'm still hopeful we can get some younger people involved." Ernie gestured towards the lounge door, from where they could hear faint humming as Rosanne busied herself with some task or other in another part of the bungalow.

"Rosanne definitely wants to be involved. She has the powers, I know. But I'm not so sure about Tommy."

Susie responded: "It's not as if we're recruiting members of a coven. This is a one-off but very important ritual. We can't be too choosy. As long as they take it seriously ..."

"That's my point." Edith butted in, "I'm not sure Tommy would take it seriously."

"Anyway" said Ernie, "To get back to the ritual. As I see it, if we all join hands in a straight line across the circle, those near the centre of the line would do the rushing, whereas those near the ends would amble at a more sedate pace and those of us right at the ends of the line wouldn't have to move at all."

"Rather like a skipping rope?" Susie interjected.

"I was thinking" said Gerald, "that it sounded a bit like the Hokey Cokey!"

"Yes, Gerald" responded Edith, "a bit like the Hokey Cokey, but with a rather more serious purpose."

"That sounds like the sort of thing we need to practise."

"Yes, we would definitely need a run-through of it all before the ritual itself, when everyone was present."

"Then it's all settled," Edith stood up and smiled as Ernie and Susie made ready to leave. "I think all that remains is to notify our guests of the time and place to meet."

"And Mum's the word, everybody." Ernie tapped his nose and winked furtively to Edith at the front door.

Noticing her nosy neighbour, Ruth, walking up the road towards them with bags full of shopping, Edith supressed a sigh and ushered the Masons away with a quick wave before Ruth could waylay them.

"Afternoon, Ruth." She called cheerily as the woman next-door ogled curiously before going into her own house.

Edith returned to her living room and sat down with a heavy sigh. "That woman knows something's afoot, I'm certain of it," she told Gerald. "She's enquired more than once about my late night visitors."

"Oh dear, and what did you tell her?" Gerald looked worried and she giggled.

"Top secret Home Guard, need-to-know basis. I know it's mean of me, but she really is a nosy old -"

"Edith!" Gerald's neat moustache bobbed up and down, as astonished as the rest of his face. "I thought you wouldn't tolerate such language in this house!"

~ TWENTY-FIVE ~

Raising the Power

Friday 2nd August 1940

The anticipated hour had come around and Gerald rushed to grab his overcoat, hat and gloves from their place in the hallway and almost forgot his small bag in his haste. As he locked his front door, he heard a hushed whisper from the road. He glanced across to see Ernie motioning for him to hurry.

"Jolly well get a move on, would you, old chap?" Ernie hissed as Gerald got to the car and climbed into the seat behind Susie, who was sitting in the front passenger seat, with a large leather satchel perched on her lap.

"Less of the old, now." he replied. "The others are meeting us there, I assume?"

"Yes, the traditional Meeting Place: that's our beloved old Naked Man tree."

Gerald leaned forward nosily to poke at the satchel Susie clutched in her hands. "What's in the bag?"

"Just a little something to help us all focus on the enemy target." She smiled cheekily. "Don't worry; you'll soon find out."

The car bumped and rattled along the roads and Susie squeaked at a jolt. "I know you've spent some time tinkering with the engine, Ernie, but are you sure the car is going to get us there in one piece?"

"Have faith, dear." he said simply.

Ernie steered the car down a narrow lane with woodlands on either side and pulled to a stop in a lay-by where one or two other cars were parked neatly out of the road and, Gerald spotted, two bicycles resting side by side against the wooden fence that ran along the edge of the narrow grass verge.

Looking around him as he got out of the vehicle, Gerald could see a small group of people in amongst the few trees that sparsely populated this part of the forest. There were over a dozen others already gathered, chief amongst them was the witch herself, busy holding court with the rest of the group hanging onto her every word while Rosamund Sabine, looking very much like the matriarch of this rag-tag band of witches, perched herself delicately on a shooting-stick seat and surveyed her little brood with quiet reflection and a watchful eye.

Gerald ambled over with Ernie and Susie to join the group and was immediately welcomed into the fold by Edith, breaking away from her conversation to administer swift hugs to them all.

"Glad you're here." Edith said, pushing a lock of hair blown loose from her hat back into place. "Did you bring the things I asked you to?"

"Right here," Gerald patted his bag. If he was not very much mistaken, there was a nervous anticipation in the air and he looked from face to face, nodding at a few people in recognition.

"Well in that case, now that we are all here, let's gather ourselves and drive a little further. The ritual site itself is in the vicinity."

***

"The car that Kitty came in looked most impressive. I think it was a Rolls Royce or a Bentley or something. I didn't know that Mr. Lawrie could afford anything like that! Still, they've arrived. Indeed, I think we've got everyone except Rosanne and Tommy. I wonder where they can have got to? I wish they'd agreed to come with me. Now I have a feeling they're not going to come at all. Still, everyone else is here, except Byngham and the blacksmith."

"Oh, Byngham's here already, over there." Susie said to Edith. "He was one of the first to arrive. He knew exactly where to come to. He knows the Forest well, after all."

"What about the blacksmith? He said he'd make his own way here. I wouldn't know who he was. I think Kitty's the only one who's met him."

"Well, look over there!" Susie pointed to a clump of trees in the middle distance.

"I can't see anything, except a New Forest pony sheltering under the trees."

"Look again!"

"That does seem a rather big pony. Oh, look. It's a horse! The blacksmith has come on a horse! I suppose that's to be expected." Edith said.

"It's certainly an old tradition." Gerald agreed, though he wondered what other surprises this evening would hold. "I have often come across stories of the witches 'borrowing' and riding a horse to their rituals, and then riding back again afterwards. There are tales of horses seeming exhausted in the morning after their night ride, the hair of their manes ragged and tangled with sweat."

Edith was too distracted to pay much attention to anyone and scanned the small gathering to see if she could pick out the blacksmith. The late hour and dark, overgrown foliage of the forest made it difficult to see much of anything at all.

"Ah! I think that must be him talking to Kitty." Charles Loader, having settled his horse, had joined Katherine Oldmeadow and that, thought Edith, meant everyone was present.

Edith tucked her hand into the crook of Gerald's elbow and squeezed his arm. He looked fondly at her and gave a small smile, lending the usual air of mischief to his eyes. She leaned her head briefly on his shoulder and he couldn't resist planting a small, chaste kiss on her forehead before she moved away to rally the troop of witches.

The trek across the bumpy terrain continued, rather slowly to make sure nobody stumbled along the way, with darkening skies and heightened gossip as they reached the appointed place, and Edith shushed everyone's eager chattering with a hiss.

"I say, listen up everybody." She glanced around and about, making quite certain they were alone among the trees and shrubs. "You all know what to do. Now let's get everything arranged and then we can begin."

"Which way are we facing?" One woman asked and Edith pointed to the North while others in the group started to place all manner of ritual items carefully in a circle large enough to contain seventeen dancing witches and a small fire.

Gerald helped Susie unwrap the parcel she brought out of her satchel and guffawed in delight when she revealed its contents. A newspaper clipping in a small, glass-frame, a photograph of the face of their enemy: Hitler, in full military dress, hand raised in his customary salute. Gerald held it up for all to see and drew attention to it.

"Look at this, now, see what Susie's got for us."

He placed the framed picture on the make-shift altar, a stubby stump of a tree in the north-east of the circle, where Edith and Rosamund were filling a goblet and plate with the usual cakes and wine.

"No, not like that," Edith remarked. She took the photograph from him and turned it around so that the Führer's face was directed towards the South-East, facing out of the circle. "We don't want him looking towards us, do we? We must position the picture so that he is facing towards the sea; we have to turn his sight away from Britain."

"Gerald, over here." Ernie and Susie called to him. "Why don't you take over the fire for us? Make sure the flames don't get too high, we can't risk being seen."

The fire was a small one in the south-east of the circle, and the energy in the Cone of Power would be directed in that direction - the direction they thought that Hitler would be in.

"We're quite in the middle of nowhere, I doubt we shall be seen." Susie replied, but Gerald crouched down to tend the fire, quite pleased to be given a role.

"True enough," Ernie agreed, "but we can't afford any interruptions, not even from any late-night poachers. This ritual is simply too important to be disturbed."

"He's right, you know," Edith agreed. "You're our fire-warden, Gerald."

She peered up above the high tree branches to take in the darkening sky and either by coincidence or something more, she and Rosamund turned to each other at the same moment and Rosamund nodded. "It's time."

Edith trotted nimbly to the boundary of the circle and began to take off her clothing and rub thick grease into her skin. That had been Gerald's idea, using thick grease to keep out the cold. She hoped it would do the trick, for it was certainly chilly this evening. Several others were busy hanging coats from branches and putting shoes and clothes where they would easily be found in the darkness later. There were a few exceptions to this, particularly the Sabines and Dorothy Fordham, but Edith did not object. She hadn't expected them to participate fully and appreciated their support from the side-lines.

"Not only is this ritual of vital importance," Edith's voice rang out clearly in the night air, "it could well be the single most important ceremony any of us ever have or shall take part in. We must put everything into this that we possibly can, we must will it with every fibre of our souls, and we shall not stop the charge of power until we are absolutely certain we have turned them away."

Looking sternly at each member of the gathered circle in turn, Edith tried to convey confidence and determination. It was the first time she had been involved in organising a large gathering with such a grand purpose, and this troubled her a little, for she was concerned her shaking hands and wavering voice might give her away.

She faced the fire-pit and began to circle slowly, arms spread wide, around the perimeter of the site. As she walked, the rest of the group fell into anticipatory silence and arranged themselves in a circle within the boundary marked out in brushwood.

The atmosphere changed in an instant and Gerald found himself, once again, in awe of her presence, her ability to capture the attention at a single, unspoken signal. He stood naked, skin tingling with anticipation, with two more witches on either side of him, both women. Man, woman, man, woman, all around the circle. This was it, he told himself, this was the moment of the greatest ritual the British Isles had seen in over a hundred years. It was time for the witches of Britain to make their stand against the German invasion.

He felt a twinge in his stomach, a bubbling, stirring sensation and he tried to calm it down by focusing on the witch. Ernie approached the altar and from it he picked up a great sword, ornately embellished and polished to high shine, which he passed with a kiss to Edith. She glanced to the side, gave a short nod, and then walked the boundary of the circle, invoking power and energy to form the magic circle.

All seventeen of them turned as one to face each of the compass points of the circle in turn to acknowledge the elemental forces; first east for air, then south for fire, west for water and finally north for earth. With every direction, Gerald observed a faint flickering of something in the air, some ethereal, almost-seen power that shimmered like heat haze as the athame, the sacred knife, was held aloft and a short invocation rang out in Edith's dramatic voice.

"Oh, great powers of air in the east, mighty ones of the watchtowers of the element of air, we beseech thee! Lend thy powers unto our spell this night, give voice and action to our magic rite!"

Gerald watched, entranced, as the witch raised her hands and the same shimmer seemed to spark between her fingers. He shivered with the rising atmosphere of magical power as the circle was completed; despite the grease that covered his naked flesh, his skin broke out in goose-pimples. He remembered his appointed task was to keep a watch on the small fire and he went over to it now, prodding and poking with a stick at the burning wood to stoke the flames. The crackle and spitting of sparks and flame added to the drama of the night, casting shadows that leaped and jumped.

From his vantage point by the fire, he took note of everything that was happening and a feeling of great pride overcame him, watching Edith in the starlight, standing tall and proud. At her signal, everyone began to circle, slowly, slowly. A drum beat joined the whispers of the rustling trees. Ba-boom, ba-boom, stamp, stamp. Bare feet, cold from the forest floor, trod down purposefully with each of the thumping beats. Slowly, slowly, the witches walked with determination, round and round, pacing, raising power with the motion of their bodies, drawing strength down from the heavens, the plethora of stars in the Milky Way, hidden by overhead branches, into the circle. A strong urge to join them all was suddenly overwhelming, and Gerald stoked the fire once again, adding a couple of branches to keep it going, and then he rose and took his place among the witches.

Catching his eye, Edith nodded briefly but did not pay him any more attention than that; she was far too occupied now with the ritual, urging the circling witches to pick up the pace. The drum beat grew faster, the swift walk became a sprightly jogging, dancing gait and still the witch urged them on. Dancing, chanting, dancing, circling.

"Raise the power, faster now!"

~ TWENTY-SIX ~

Sending Forth

Friday 2nd August 1940

Edith's skin broke out in goose-flesh in protest against the cool night air and her breath came in short, ragged gasps. She gave the pre-arranged signal and the group quickly organised themselves into a long line. Facing the direction of the sea, a pulsing wave of magical energy surged out of them all as they raced forward. They cried out in unison as they had rehearsed, crying to the stars, the heavens, the Gods themselves.

"Can't cross the sea, can't cross the sea!"

A spike of tree bark fallen on the grass pricked the sole of her foot, but she ignored the sharp, fleeting pain and darted swiftly, her hands clasping those of the witches next to her, urging them on. Rich and heady incense fumes rose from each quarter of the circle, mixing with the smoke of the fire to create a pungent aroma that she breathed in deeply.

"Again," Edith urged them on, a force for good running towards the direction of their enemy, directing their thoughts and the power they had raised straight to the mind of the Führer to disrupt his vile plans.

The trees that surrounded their sacred space were rustling audibly, as though they too were joining in, adding their voices to the melee.

"Not able to come, not able to come!"

"Again!" She called out loudly, fierce determination and grit etched into every face. They were building up power and energy in a great magical vortex that was already stronger than any she had known before but still she whipped them up into a faster pace, a louder chant.

"Can't cross the sea!"

She caught sight of Hitler's photograph, facing in the direction of the ocean, and used it as her focus. This was the man who threatened their peace, this was the face of their enemy. He could not, would not, bring his army to the shores of Britain with their ships and their tanks and their guns. She gritted her teeth, feeling the power growing stronger and stronger.

"NOW!" She was standing in the centre of the line, holding hands tightly with those on either side of her, and with a final, heart-felt call, Edith rushed forwards for a fourth and final time. Pulling the line with her, feeling the support and power of the coven joining her. She ran and ran, summoning every bit of her internal strength.

"CAN'T CROSS THE SEA!" She screamed it out and sixteen other voices yelled it with her. Every one of them full of grim determination and power, they called out, this cacophony of witches.

"Not able to come, not able to come!"

She pointed deliberately ahead, directing the magic, so clear to her she could actually see it; a haze of misty light that flowed from her body, from all of them, through their arms and out of their hands, rushing off to do its work. Now her body was still, the energy had peaked and was on its way, but still she remained with her arms outstretched, chest rising visibly with quickened breath, and willed all her concentration and focus towards the sea.

And then, suddenly, she knew it was done.

Almost as one, the others started to lower their hands and she followed suit, spent. They were all exhausted, she realised, as she broke away from the hands of her fellow witches, for in this single moment of magic they were all witches. One by one, they broke the line and rested, at last.

Gerald especially seemed to be struggling to catch his breath and he leaned forward, hands on his knees while he drew in wisps of air that wheezed audibly. Edith glanced at the assembly of witches. There were barely three of them under forty years old and most were much older. This ritual, the amount of effort put into it by all, and the energy it expended, had visibly taken its toll and she wondered, briefly, if that was to be the price of it.

It must work. For all of this to be worth it, it had to.

ACT THREE

CONSEQUENCES

~ TWENTY-SEVEN ~

Edith Solves Rosanne's Worries

Monday 5th August 1940

"Mother" said Rosanne, "I know that ritual took it out of you, but it is not much more than a week until my wedding and there are so many things we haven't thought about yet."

"My dear, you may not have thought about them, but I can assure you that I have."

"But you haven't even started making my wedding dress. We're going to run out of time!"

"I'm sorry, but I couldn't get the material to make a traditional dress. Have you forgotten there's a war on? We'll have to think of an alternative."

"It seems to me that the only alternative would be to go skyclad. That would be bound to please the members of the naturist club at any rate, though it would be a shock the Reverend Brownlow."

"Rosanne, don't be absurd. But to be serious for a moment, the only thing I can think of is that you wear the going-away outfit that I made for you. It's really an afternoon dress, but you like the light brown colour, don't you? And we can make it special by adding a hat. I'm sure I've got one that will do. And if you hold a spray of pink carnations, it would look quite elegant. I'm sorry, Rosanne, but we are going through difficult times."

"Yes, I do appreciate that, mother, and all that you are doing. We must all compromise, I suppose. It is wartime after all."

"Anyway", Edith continued, "It will be nice having the wedding service in the Priory rather than St. Mark's. I was speaking to

Henry Brownlow only the other day and he is looking forward to conducting the ceremony for you. So that's one less thing to worry about."

"Thank you, mother!" Rosanne came over and leant her head on Edith's shoulder. "And you've organised the reception?"

"Yes, I spoke to various members of the naturist club last time I was there, and they recommended the Nelson Hotel next to the club. I've spoken to the landlord and in normal times, they could have supplied all the food, but now he suggested the easiest thing would be for everyone to bring contributions of food. The pub, I assume, would supply drinks as usual. Oh, and he's got a cardboard wedding cake."

"Cardboard? I absolutely refuse to eat cardboard!"

"No dear, there will be a proper cake, of course, but it won't be very big, and it'll be a rather plain affair. The cardboard one will be just for show. It'll look good in the photographs. It's all the rage to have a cardboard wedding cake these days!"

"If you say so, mother. If you say so." Rosanne pouted but resigned herself to it.

Edith shifted her position and raised another point, something that had been on her mind for some time. "It's normal for the bride's father to give her away and I wrote to your father some time ago but haven't heard anything. It sounds like he doesn't want to have anything to do with it."

"That's no surprise. Well, I don't see why I have to be given away. I'm nobody's possession. I'm my own woman."

"We all know that, but we have to make some concession to orthodoxy. How would you like to be given away by Gerald?"

"What a wonderful idea." Rosanne jumped up to give her mother a hug. "I do hope he will agree to it, I think I've become as fond of him as you have."

"And I know he adores you. What's more, I happen to know that he's planning to give you a substantial sum of money as a wedding present."

"He's a very generous man, isn't he? It always surprises me where he got his money."

"Don't ask, dear. Don't ask," said Edith, hurriedly changing the subject. "And I know you can't afford to have a lavish honeymoon, but I telephoned my friend, Kate, in Glastonbury, and she can put you both up in her spare room for a week or so. Would you like that?"

"Oh, that would be nice, thank you, Mother. We can take Tommy's sports car, so we would be able to drive around in the vicinity of Glastonbury."

"Then it's settled and when you return, I shall have made my move to Avenue Cottage, and you and Tommy will have Theano to yourselves. Your first home together, as you start your married life; you must be excited."

Rosanne was silent for a moment. "You do think I'm doing the right thing, don't you mother, in marrying Tommy?"

Edith pondered, "I'm hardly the one to be giving you advice, considering the relationship, or lack thereof, that I had with your father. I expect you guessed that we never really got the hang of it. There was such a shortage of men after the last war that I was rather indiscriminate in my choice of husband."

"Do you think it might be hereditary, mother?"

"I don't know, dear. I really don't know."

Saturday 10th August 1940

CHRISTCHURCH TIMES

NEW FOREST PROMISES A "SPITFIRE"

HIGHCLIFFE PLAYS ITS PART

VILLAGES THROUGHOUT THE NEW FOREST HAVE EMBARKED UPON A BIG EFFORT TO RAISE BETWEEN £5,000 AND £6,000 TO PROVIDE A SPITFIRE FIGHTER.

The effort is sponsored by the Hon. Mrs. Pleydell-Bouverie, of Palace House, Beaulieu, and Mrs. L. Shennan, of "Oldways," Beaulieu, daughter of the late Sir Thomas Troubridge, a former President of the New Forest Association, has undertaken the duties of hon. secretary.

The area covered within the scheme is that of the New Forest and Christchurch Parliamentary Constituency, and is being run apart from, but in harmony with, the Hampshire Campaign, organised by Dr. H. King, of Bournemouth.

Each village is being asked to make a contribution and village or district committees are being set up to facilitate the collection of funds.

At Highcliffe a committee has been formed under the chairmanship of the Hon. Mrs. Stuart Wortley, C.B.E. Mrs. R. Turner, of "St. Mary's," Walkford, is acting as hon. secretary, Mr. J. H. Darwin, "Sterle House," Highcliffe, hon. treasurer.

~ TWENTY-EIGHT ~

An Unexpected Sadness

Monday 12th August 1940

The moment Edith opened the door and saw Gerald's face, she knew that something was wrong.

"Edith, I'll come straight to the point. I have some very sad news for you." He hesitated for a few moments and ushered her into her living room to sit down. "I'm afraid Walter Forder is dead. He died on Sunday. It was a heart attack. I felt I had to come and tell you in person."

"Oh dear, how terrible. Poor, dear Walter. I am afraid our ritual may have contributed to his heart-attack."

"Yes, it brings it home to you, doesn't it? You do know that my asthma has come back? It was very bad when I was little. When I started working in Ceylon, it became less severe until gradually, it left me entirely. For my whole working life Out East, there was no sign of it. And after I came back to England, I thought I had been cured. Until the day of the ritual, when it came back with a vengeance. The only way I can get any sleep at all now is to sit up in bed. I hope it will diminish in intensity as the days pass, but I suspect it will be with me now until the day I die."

"I'm so sorry to hear that, and about Walter, I know you were well acquainted."

"We are none of us in our prime, Daff. Perhaps Walter was not capable of handling the power we raised that night, all that charging about in the forest."

The witch stood up, her shoes clacking lightly on the wooden floorboards. He watched her as she went to the window, resting her forehead on the glass as the world carried on outside without a care for the passing of their friend.

"He was, magically speaking, as capable as you or I. That ritual took it out of all of us. I believe it worked, but I'm afraid that what we wanted to achieve and the sheer power of the magic we needed to make it happen was so tremendous and great that... Well, the truth of it is that what we were asking was a massive undertaking, with all kinds of opposing and powerful forces working against us."

"And that leaves those of us who are left to continue fighting in whatever ways we are able to."

"I am putting my foot down, we cannot repeat what we have done. We cannot put our people at further risk and there are other things we can do to contribute. I know that dear Dorothy has massively contributed to the Spitfire fund and that Rosamund, though she didn't admit it, may have done the same. I don't know what more I can possibly do myself, though, I am wrung through and worn out."

He raised his head and met her doleful, solemn eyes. He could almost hear the words before she said them.

"There was a price to pay, Gerald, for what we did. I believe it demanded something from us."

"What the devil are you saying?" Gerald struck his fist hard on the table, with anger or with grief, he wasn't sure which. "Walter? A sacrifice? Is that it, Dafo? A sacrifice for the greater good?"

Edith swung round to face him, her head high. "You believe it too, don't you?" Her voice so quiet it sent a chill up his spine. "You of all people should know about sacrifice, Gerald, with your asthma causing you problems after all those years without it."

As much as he wanted to protest, his shoulders slumped a little and he nodded. She was right. Damnable woman, she was always right. Even now, his breath came in a ragged, tight struggle accompanied by a hint of wheezing noise and he forced himself to get it under control.

~ TWENTY-NINE ~

The Magna Carta Letter

Tuesday 13th August 1940

Gerald knocked loudly on the door of Edith's little bungalow on Dennistoun Avenue, which he had come to think of as the witch's house. As he waited for a response, he noted that the little garden at the front of the property, where he locked up his bicycle, was in dire need of weeding in one corner. A plot of weeds with fern-like little leaves and whiteish coloured flowers had cropped up like a plague. Most unsightly.

The door opened and Edith ushered him through to the kitchen. "I shouldn't be surprised that you've turned up this morning. How's the asthma today?"

"Never mind all that, you have read the Telegraph?"

"'Gerald, I know quite well enough what you wish to discuss, but first we must have tea and a slice of madeira cake. Don't you agree?"

Gerald was slightly taken aback. Normally the offer of sweet treats was hard-earned at this house.

As she positioned lace doilies, plates and so forth on the table, Gerald took his own copy of the newspaper and read aloud from it.

> "Belgium and France were lost because the civilian population bolted instead of staying and delaying the invaders. It has been proved in many wars that if the civil population will fight delaying actions they can be most troublesome to invaders and may even beat them."

"Ah, yes, your letter to the editor. I already saw it, Gerald. No need to read it out on my account."

That was hardly fair, he thought, the entire content of the letter he had written to the newspaper was worthy of reading out and nobody, witch or otherwise, was about to deny him his moment in the spotlight. He continued to read loudly, waving off any further attempts on her part to shut him up.

> "It is part of German tactics to make it believed that civilians cannot, and may not, resist invaders, because the Germans well know how difficult they are to fight. In the last war the Germans encouraged civilians in East Prussia and Poland to snipe when the army had retreated.
>
> The made-in-Germany rules of war mean that Germany does not obey the rules of war as they have hitherto been understood. Why should we? Everyone willing should be given arms when they are available and taught how to use them.
>
> If the French villages had resisted, the German Motor-Cycle troops could not have come on as they did. If each village and town had defended itself, France would never have fallen as she did, and Germany might well have been on the way to defeat now.
>
> Why should people who wish to defend themselves be prevented, just to make it easy for Germany? By Magna Carta every free-born Englishman is entitled to have arms to defend himself and his household. Let us now claim our right."

There was a silence then and Gerald knew he was being watched carefully by the witch. After a while, she said: "I am sure it pleases you to see your letter in the paper, but what good does it do? It's not as if Churchill will respond to you and say, 'why, Mister Gardner, how right you are! We shall send munitions to householders this very instant!"

He was about to interject but she gave no pause. "If the resources were available, perhaps our local defence would be better equipped, but there aren't sufficient provisions to go around."

Gerald let her have her say while he tucked into another piece of madeira cake and then he replied, "that's exactly where I come in. You have seen my rather extensive collection, of course."

"Your collection of - of weaponry? Oh Gerald, do you really intend to lend out all those precious knives, swords and what-not to the Local Defence Volunteers? I mean, the Home Guard."

"I intend to do exactly that. As I make plain in my letter, *everyone willing should be given arms when they are available and taught how to use them!* Well, my armoury is available and so the people will be given arms and if necessary, I shall train them myself. I have spoken about this at length with Major Fish already. We had a blast - quite literally - some months ago, as you know, and I am sure my contributions will be well received."

Edith laughed out loud at that and Gerald scowled at her playfully. "I don't know what is so amusing. I would be quite capable of giving instruction to the young whipper-snappers, and the older ones too. I may not be fit enough to fight myself, but my mind is sharp."

"You must do as you please, of course. You normally do."

"In that case, I shall help myself to more cake, if you don't mind."

Edith pulled the plate out of his reach, however, and looked at him reproachfully. "No, I am sorry, Gerald, but I must insist if you keep eating me out of all the sweet things in the house, especially so close to Rosanne's wedding, that you try and find me more eggs. Susie has promised to bring some for me, not that we are strictly allowed to give our rations to anybody else of course, but if you do have any to spare, it'll make the wedding cake stretch a little further among the guests."

'I think I could manage that," Gerald said, and this time when he reached for another slice of cake, Edith obliged and let him have it.

"While you're here, Gerald," Edith said, "we must talk about the wedding. I want your assurances that you won't turn up in your short trousers and socks with sandals."

"Don't worry." He replied, wiping crumbs from his fingers. "I shall be on my very best behaviour and I have a nice outfit in mind that even you won't object to."

~ THIRTY ~

The Fire Dims at the Forge

Thursday 15th August 1940

A gentle knock on the window disturbed her quiet reflection and self-chastisement and, looking up, she saw a familiar face peering in through the window.

"Come in." She stood up wearily and went to greet her visitor at the front door.

"Hello," she said, "What brings you here? Have a seat in the lounge and I shall make us some tea." She walked through the house towards the kitchen, followed by her guest. Turning, she was startled to see the expression on their face. Ashen white. Serious.

"What is it? Has something happened?" Suddenly her heart was pounding and she clutched her hands together with dread.

"I'm so sorry," the visitor said, their head shaking sadly from side to side. "What we did, it was too much for some us. Another member of our circle was taken ill a few days ago."

"My God, no!" The woman staggered slightly and guiding hands led her to the kitchen, gently pressing her to sit. "Is it serious?"

"I'm sorry but he died last night."

"He? Which one of them?" She raised a hand to her face, clammy and cold with fear. "Tell me who it is! Have I lost him? Is it him?"

"I'm afraid it's Charles Loader. Apparently, he shod his last horse the day before the ritual and was not in good health at all after we did it."

Hit by a wave of relief that Gerald's asthma had not snatched him away from her, Edith let the news sink in. Blacksmith to the gypsy community, whisperer of the Horseman's Word, Charles Loader had seemed in fine health before the ritual, she remembered that clearly. She also remembered how exhausted she herself had been in the immediate aftermath. Had she been wrong, she wondered now, to talk so idly with Ernie and the others about sacrifice?

"Oh dear, I shall have to tell Gerald. He will be most upset, he was very excited at meeting Charles. I think they talked about him visiting the forge, some mutual discussions and cooing over metal work apparently."

"Must be like wise-women," Rosamund muttered, "we always recognise each other at a glance and can't help but gather together."

"When will it stop, Rosamund? First Walter, now Charles, and poor Gerald is in a bad way with his asthma and I fear for him. When will it stop?"

"Gerald will survive all right, I assure you. And I believe we have achieved our objective - to have stopped Hitler in his tracks. There's nothing more we can do now. You concentrate on your daughter's wedding. That will be something positive to keep your mind occupied."

~ THIRTY-ONE ~

Rosanne and Tommy Tie the Knot

Saturday 17th August 1940

Rosanne's wedding day was a far smaller and less luxurious affair than Edith would have liked for her only daughter, but in these trying times, she had done the best possible job. Rosanne's friend, Alice, a trainee hair-dresser who had given up her career to work as a land-girl, had taken time off for the wedding and spent over an hour fussing with the bride's hair and make-up. Rosanne's hair, rich and glossy, curled nicely around her face and was topped with a delicate, pretty hat from Edith's extensive collection. The light brown dress she wore hugged her slim figure nicely and the fabric glinted lightly in the golden sunlight every time she swung around, and Edith thought she had never been prouder.

She hoped that today's wedding was the start of a long and happy marriage and not a disaster in waiting. Despite her best efforts to save her own failing relationship, things had become unbearable and she and her husband separated in 1938. She sent up a silent plea to the Old Gods that Rosanne did not have such bad luck. Still, Tommy was smiling broadly, she saw now, a smile that included his eyes, always a good sign, she reckoned.

"I thought you promised Rosanne you weren't going to cry?" Gerald put his arm around her waist and handed a handkerchief to her.

"I did say that, didn't I?" Edith sniffed, "yet here I am in need of a handkerchief because I cried anyway."

"Just as we both knew you would." He chuckled and put his hand over her shoulders, guiding her towards the top table where they took their place beside Rosanne and Tommy.

"Are you ready?" she turned to Gerald with a smile. He nodded and stood up, chinking a spoon against the side of a glass.

"Dear friends," he began, "it is my great honour that young Rosanne has invited me to provide the toast at her wedding to Tommy. I'd like to start by saying how very pleased it makes me …"

Knowing this could go on for some time, Gerald being an enthusiastic and engaging speaker, Edith inclined her head toward Rosanne and whispered.

"You look so very lovely, darling, Tommy too, in his suit. I do hope you will both be happy. Happier than I was with your father."

"I am happy, Mother."

After the speeches, the bride and groom posed for a photograph, along with Edith, of course, and Gerald too. The cardboard cake was there for show and after the photographs were taken, the proper cake was brought out and there was enough for all of the guests to have a small piece, thanks to the cautious use of sugar and eggs over the last couple of weeks along with a gratefully received package from Susie, who had saved her rations to add to the cake batter.

Edith decided there and then that she would have to find a suitable gift for Susie, who had helped out quite considerably with the wedding preparations, not only by saving the eggs, but decorating the function room with bunting and ribbons to cheer it up and generally being on hand for any last-minute jobs. The addition of hundreds of rose petals, taken carefully from Edith's own rose garden and dried out over the last several days, was a nice finishing touch and that had been Susie's idea. Perhaps a piece of jewellery might be a nice gift, she thought, and immediately a delicate gold bracelet in her collection sprang to mind. It was one which she had received herself as a thank-you present when she had left the service of Mrs. Waud at Ferniehurst and she thought it would suit Susie well enough.

Thinking of this and enjoying the wedding celebrations had set her in a very fine mood and she smiled fondly at Gerald as he took time to shake hands with people and exchange pleasantries. He had become such a dear friend, and she rather wished they had met years ago. Her life to this point would have been very different if he had been part of it.

"What are you smiling at?" Rosanne was suddenly beside her and Edith shook her head.

"It's nothing, dear." She said, turning her attention away from Gerald, but not before Rosanne could follow her gaze and guess what thoughts had been on her mind.

"Ah, I see." Rosanne nodded. "Never mind, you may not have the right circumstances in this life-time but I know both of you believe there will be another life after this one comes to an end. Perhaps when you are reincarnated you shall know one another again and things will turn out differently."

"What a thought!" Edith could think of nothing else to say on the subject. Instead, she pulled Rosanne towards the table where drinks were being served and helped them both to a glass of wine. "Tell me, darling, have you always been this shrewd and I didn't notice until now or has married life started working its magic on you already?"

~ THIRTY-TWO ~

Another Witch on Avenue Road

Friday 23rd August 1940

Edith carefully took her best china set out of a large, heavy box, unwrapped the layers of newspaper she had wrapped around each piece, and stowed the set in the kitchen sideboard. The removal firm had not needed a large van, as much of the furniture at the bungalow on Dennistoun Avenue would remain there for Rosanne and Tommy to make use of. However, there were several boxes of kitchenware, her favourite chair and footstool, furniture for the bedroom and dozens of books, ornaments and personal belongings. She had packed everything herself, rather time consuming in the midst of wedding celebrations and ritual preparation, but worth the effort to ensure nothing became damaged or misplaced. Every crate and box had been meticulously labelled and the two fellows who did the actual lifting and shifting had placed each one in its correct place in the house before they left, leaving her alone in the silent house, surrounded by belongings to be put in their place.

Avenue Cottage was grander than Theano, the bungalow in Somerford, and the garden was considerably bigger. Here, on Avenue Road, Edith was nearly within shouting distance of Rosamund and George Sabine's property, Whinchat, and only a matter of streets away from Gerald's house on Highland Avenue.

It would be very convenient for them both to continue their friendship and no doubt they would call on one another even more frequently now. She could take one of two routes - the first one being more direct, from the end of Avenue Road, a short cut through Chewton Common which led directly to Bracken Way, and then to Highland Avenue. It would be more pleasant, she mused, to take the second option and walk the full length of the common, picking up Elphinstone Road and then turning right onto Highland Avenue.

Chewton Common was popular with dog-walkers, thick with trees, bracken and brambles. If she took a basket with her on each trip back and forth, there would be all kinds of plants and berries to forage for, especially at this time of year. Blackberry pies, crab-apple jelly, herb butters, wild salad leaves - the tastes and scents of the wood were almost tangible. With her mind now full of the wide range of medicinal and culinary produce she was likely to find virtually on her door-step, Edith decided on a whim that after a long day of hard-work organising her new home, she deserved a break.

Now, where were her wicker baskets? The house was still in disarray and she searched the ground floor, finding only the smallest of her baskets. It would have to suffice; she was eager to get outside into the fresh air while the mood was still with her. The air outdoors was cool and the sky full of pale, fluffy grey clouds, cirrocumulus, if her memory was correct.

Avenue Road was not long, and she soon reached the footpath leading through the common and ambled happily along, stopping here and there to pick the first of the early blackberries, adding them to her basket along with the narrow, feathered leaves of yarrow. A chaffinch called out above her, startled by her intrusion in his woodland home.

She was startled herself just then, as she saw a familiar figure walking along the rough path towards her from the opposite direction, waving cheerily.

"Edith, how lovely to see you here." Rosamund was wearing a smart tweed skirt and jacket and looked very neat, though on her feet were a pair of wellington boots rather than every-day shoes. Like Edith, she had a wicker basket over one arm, half-full of leafy green plants.

"Likewise," Edith smiled, "though I suppose I shouldn't be surprised really. We are virtually neighbours now, after all. What have you found?"

"Yarrow, some wild raspberry leaves, white-flowered dead-nettle, not flowering now, of course, and the leaves are larger and older than I'd like, but still useful - you know what these are all for, I expect."

"I certainly do," Edith was very familiar with those particular plants, "a soothing tincture for ladies, by the sound of it."

Rosamund nodded, giving Edith her seal of approval. "Very good. Modern wise-women such as ourselves must make full use of our foraging skills, especially as this frightful war continues to make everything so dreadfully hard to get hold of."

"Quite right." Edith agreed.

"Nature provides such a bounty, right under our noses, don't you agree, dear?"

She nodded politely, wondering what else her fellow herbalist had in that basket, but as she craned her neck to see, Rosamund discreetly rearranged herself to obscure the view.

"Well, it has been delightful to bump into you, Edith, but I must be on my way." Rosamund declared. "Do call in soon, won't you?"

Edith smiled and continued on her way, adding raspberry and dead-nettle leaves to her own basket as she came across them. Although her curiosity was piqued, she decided it wouldn't have been right to press old Mother Sabine on the matter of her mystery plants and what they might be used for. After all, what wise-woman or herbalist did not have a few secrets of her own to keep.

176

~ THIRTY-THREE ~

'Highcliffe Resident Annoys Nazis'

Saturday 24th August 1940

After the support he had received in response to his letter to the Telegraph earlier in the week, Gerald was excited to see another report at the weekend, this time in the Christchurch Times. He was pleased to receive word from Ernie, who wished to discuss the matter with him, and the two of them arranged to meet for high-tea at a café in Christchurch. Ernie had arrived first and had two newspapers on the seat beside him, the table taken up with cups and saucers and a pot of tea.

"You are becoming quite the media personality, my friend." Ernie said, while Gerald made himself comfortable at the table. He began to read from the Christchurch Times.

Highcliffe Resident Annoys Nazis

Today's Frankfurter Zeitung, in a prominent front-page cable from Berlin, rants against the writer of the letter and the conditions in which it obtained publicity. The writer must know, says the cable, that human ethics have advanced in the last 700 years. His suggestion is condemned as medieval and as an infringement of international law.

It is obvious from the whole German press, and also from official reactions, that the spirit of the English people is entirely unexpected and most discomforting to the Nazis.

It seemed that Gerald had set the cat among the pigeons, a feat which pleased him enormously. Though he did not like to deliberately annoy people, and his actions and well-placed words were never intended to harm anyone, he did like to ruffle a few feathers in high places if he could and in this case, it was justified.

"You were mentioned in The Telegraph again on the 22nd August," Ernie stabbed one of the newspapers with his finger to make his point, "and New Milton was bombed later that very day. Now here you are again in the Christchurch Times." Ernie indicated the second newspaper that sat between them.

"What of it?" Gerald retorted, sitting quite upright in his chair and looking at Ernie with suspicion. "My letter to the editor and the subsequent bombing are two separate things, absolutely unconnected."

"If you hadn't written that letter that annoyed Hitler, this would never have happened," Ernie said, "or so some folk would say."

"Germany ruthlessly disregarded the international laws. They can no longer plead what was right or not right!"

"Well, whether urged on by your letter or not, Gerald," Ernie conceded, "the consequences are such that..."

"The consequences, Ernie, are not a result of any letter to the Telegraph, whatever people around here may think. Hitler has it in for us all and it should come as a surprise to no-one that he has given the orders to start direct attacks. New Milton is positioned right on the coast, just as we are here. And - oh, excuse me."

Gerald broke off in a rough fit of coughing, brought on by his quick speech and the rough, ragged breathing of an asthma attack. Ernie patted him on the back and watched worriedly until the attack passed and Gerald managed, thankfully, to get his breathing back under control.

"Nearly scared me half to death there, old man."

"Less of the 'old man', if you don't mind." Gerald held up out a hand and Ernie helped him from his seat. "I shall have to go and get some rest, I think. We can carry this on another time, Ernie."

"I shall go back with you," Ernie offered.

"If you insist." Gerald would normally scoff at such an idea but with the loss of his two pals still fresh in his mind, even he conceded that Ernie's caution was wise. "And not a word of this to Edith, she frets enough as it is."

~ THIRTY-FOUR ~

But Did It Work?

Monday 16th September 1940

Gerald arrived at Avenue Cottage and Edith showed him to the sitting room. However, he was a little disappointed to see that Ernie and Susie were also here, side-by-side on the couch. He had been looking forward to having Dafo all to himself for a time.

"Ah, good afternoon to you." He took up residence in a dark brown leather armchair by the window of the sitting room. "Now, what is this all about? I had not anticipated you two both joining us here."

"Ernie and Susie, and you too, Gerald, were all so very helpful during my recent move that I thought a formal invitation to tea would be in order now that I'm settled in and feeling at home."

Gerald sensed that this was not the only reason behind her invitation. He wondered if he was becoming more psychic as a result of his studies and practice and therefore able to pick up on this or if it was simply that his close friendship with Edith meant that he sensed her brooding mood.

"I do like to entertain, as you all know by now, but in addition to that I thought it was high time we had a proper debriefing following our ritual."

"What is there to say?" Gerald posed the question. "Hitler has high-tailed it, we've sent him packing."

"How can you say that," Edith sounded cross, "after the air raid on London just a week ago? I heard the planes, in fact. They passed right overhead with such a racket and in all honesty, I can't say that I wasn't frightened."

"I heard them too," said Gerald, "and it isn't over yet, but they still haven't breached our shores. Their plans to invade by sea have come to naught."

"Correct, and that was our specific aim. Now, is that because our magical efforts were effective?" Ernie asked the friends. "What do you think, Edith? You planned our ritual with very precise aims. Is it coincidental that Hitler has cancelled his plans to cross the sea? A result of some other set of circumstances?"

"These matters are never clear-cut, Ernie, you know that," she helped herself to a sandwich as they talked, "I believe that across the etheric planes - the astral, if you like - we sent our magical energies directly into his mind. Hitler heard our message loud and clear: he was not welcome on our shores."

"I could certainly feel some kind of - oh, I can't describe it." Susie's voice was full of frustration. "We don't have the right words to express it. All I can say is that I felt the magical energy building and building up to a crescendo. As we rushed forward when the power was at its greatest, there was a sensation of completion. As if everything we had been working towards was carried out."

"That's my intuition too," Edith concurred, "that we did indeed send forth our power and it hit the target."

"Incredible." Gerald stood up with an enthusiastic leap. "Marvellous," he cried out and clapped his hands together, a broad smile on his face, "simply marvellous. We actually reached Hitler!"

"Yes, we did it all right." Ernie agreed. "The witches of Britain are not to be trifled with, as others have found out to their cost in the past. The Spanish Armada, Napoleon, Hitler. Now there's a subject for you to write about, Gerald!"

Edith was horrified at the thought and said so vehemently. "Please, don't encourage him, Ernie. We must tell no-one and you certainly shall not put any of this into a book, for goodness' sake! We work in the shadows, we have always done so and with very good reason; the matter is closed."

"Ah yes, witchcraft doesn't pay for broken windows. That's what you told me, Edith." Gerald returned to his chair and reached to the little coffee table for another helping of tea but the pot was empty. "Things have changed somewhat, surely you can see that? We have been victorious and I think that the people of our fine country ought to know just what we witches have been doing to help the war effort."

"There will always be a threat to our kind from those who don't understand and don't care to learn what we really do. There are very good reasons why we must practise our craft with the utmost secrecy. Besides, the majority of people will simply not believe that the invasion was called off through magical means, rather than political and military ones."

"We are still under threat, though, by air." Gerald grumbled loudly. "We've done our bit, now it's over to the boys in the RAF."

Ernie tapped his fingers together thoughtfully and shook his head. "Nobody is denying that, Gerald. We did not work our magic to stop the war, nor the air raids. We worked to stop the invasion and that threat, as far as we can tell, is now virtually non-existent. I say then, that our efforts were a success."

"You said previously that you thought others might have done similar ritual workings, Ernie." Gerald said.

"Without a doubt," Ernie nodded. "Anyone with our interests would naturally wish to put their mental and psychic abilities to good use. We chose one aspect on which to focus our energies, other groups would have done their own style of work too, perhaps choosing different things on which to focus their energies."

"You mean, I suppose that, stopping the war itself is simply too great a feat. Yet it was within our power to act in a small way that has prevented the German forces coming to our shores."

"Exactly that, Edith." Ernie sat back in his chair, then sprang forwards again and pulled a clean kerchief from his breast pocket, handing it to Edith. "Whatever is the matter now?"

"I was just thinking of poor Charles Loader and Walter Forder." Edith sniffed and wiped her eyes dry. "And what a dreadful shame it is that they can't be here with us to take pride in all that we have achieved."

~ THIRTY-FIVE ~

Farewell to Friends

Thursday 31st October 1940

On the night of Samhain, they gathered, they who had taken part in that great, magical battle for Britain. There were fewer people this night, gathering in the heart of the New Forest. On this occasion, the meeting place was a stand of trees that provided some privacy, a short walk from the Naked Man tree, where bare branches gave little shelter from the drizzling rain. Edith had arrived with Gerald at twilight, when the low clouds gradually darkened and the last of the birds had fallen quiet, giving way to the soft forest noises of foxes and unseen small creatures, so that they could spend a silent time together, sharing a flask of sweet tea and talking of this and that.

With wellington boots, dark robe and umbrella, Edith contemplated all that she and her fellow witches and companions had done. Her thoughts in the first few days and weeks immediately after that last, significant and powerful ritual, had been hopeful, even though it was some time before they could be certain that there would indeed be no invasion, at least not by sea. With those doubts now gone, she knew that their great work had been successful, worthwhile and of vital importance, contributing in very real terms to the war effort. And yet, a sadness within her also knew that without their actions, for which she had been the driving force, those dear lives might not have been lost. It was not anybody's fault, but that last ritual had been dreadfully tiring, exhausting even, and there was little wonder that not all of the participants had fared well after dancing, darting and running around in the open air wearing naught but their skin. Thinking so, she sighed aloud and lifted her head up to the silent sky with a tear in her eye.

Gerald, who had been silent for a time, must have been thinking along similar lines, as he said, "Nobody could have predicted the losses we suffered, you understand. It was out of our hands."

"You're right, darling," she replied, "as you so very often are. I'm being silly and emotional when, in fact, I could have done nothing more or less than that final ritual. It was my duty, in a way, to lead everyone to do that, and they all came willingly."

"Quite so." He nodded. "Here we are, Edith, the Masons are on the way, over there."

As the Mason siblings clambered over stray branches and bracken to join Gerald and Edith in the circle, the twilight had given way to full darkness and Edith forced herself to brighten up as Ernie, Susie and Rosetta greeted them both with long hugs.

"Good to see you, old chap." Ernie and Gerald shook hands firmly, as was their custom. "Ah ha, Byngham! How are you faring?"

Harry Byngham, he thought, was looking far from well. He seemed both frail and resigned, his strength had been sapped and he had the appearance of a man who had once had great strength, a man who had given it all, or nearly all. He shook hands with Ernie and Gerald and nodded sadly.

"I'm not at my best, as you can see, but I shall make the most of things. Nothing more we can do, is there?"

"I was looking forward to becoming well acquainted with Mister Loader, you know."

"A pity you hadn't come across each other until recently, he had a wicked sense of humour."

They talked for a short while and it occurred to Gerald that he, himself, was also not at his best and the coming winter would not be at all good for his chest. With a pinch of luck, Edith or Susie might know some helpful remedy or herb that could help, but he knew from experience that it could only be eased, and not cured entirely.

"A penny for your thoughts?" Susie whispered to Edith. "You look as if you need a long, hot bath and a tot of strong whisky."

"Oh, nothing much, Susie." Edith fibbed, tucking any last traces of guilt firmly to the back of her mind. "I'm full of tears, nothing else. Did you bring those photographs I asked you to get hold of?"

"Here," Ernie reached into the breast pocket of his heavy overcoat and took out a large brown envelope which he passed to her. Inside were two black-and-white photographs: Walter Forder and Charles Loader. Ernie saw the sad expression on the witch's face and put his arm around her shoulder, but she shook him off.

"Look at me, crying like a child. That won't do at all, will it? I have to prepare the altar and - oh, Susie, look!" She had spotted movement in the darkness and pointed to where several figures were emerging. "A few more of us are arriving now. Would you help me to organise these things?"

Susie and Edith left Gerald, Ernie and Rosetta to speak to some of the others, those who had been able to make it, as they started to arrive for the ritual. They set up a small, folding table that Ernie had brought along and placed on it an assortment of candles, a jar of incense, a dish of salt water, and other ritual accoutrements.

In front of these items, the photographs were placed for all to see and although some of the ad-hoc coven were talking quietly among themselves, when Edith was satisfied that the altar was in place and everyone she expected had arrived, the gathering was at once quiet and still. Edith nodded to herself, satisfied, and around her, the small gathering, including Katherine Oldmeadow, Harry Byngham, and a few of the others who had been involved that tremendous night, looked earnestly to her, as she readied herself to begin. Now, it was all over, and those who were notable by their absence had to be honoured.

Standing tall, and looking very much the part of a regal High Priestess with her hooded cloak, Edith walked to the middle of the clearing and the rest of the group formed a circle around the edge of the space.

Edith held up one hand, finger pointing, to the boundary of the circle and walked slowly around the perimeter, directing a laser of energy to protect the space and those within it.

'This is the night of Samhain,' Edith began, 'when we pay homage and give our thanks to our ancestors, the Beloved Dead.'

The group took turns to say a few words of their own, giving respect and honour to Walter Forder and Charles Loader.

"I shall miss having a direct line to the newspapers," Gerald said, "however shall I procure reviews for my books now?" A polite but short-lived bust of soft laughter rang out before he continued. "In all seriousness, Walter had become a friend, not close, perhaps, but he had a canny intelligence, a superb memory, a clever way with words, of course, and I am sorry that we shall not have the chance to become close."

Katherine Oldmeadow came towards the candles on the little make-shift altar and held one bright, flickering light aloft. "Farewell, fellow traveller on the roads to knowledge, Charles Loader, blacksmith, farrier, friend. We shall always remember your contribution to our cause, your quick smile and helpful nature. Rest in peace, my friend."

Now it was Ernie who spoke, loudly and clearly. 'To all of those who have lost their lives, we say this: May your souls be healed in the afterlife and may you return to us swiftly in a new form so that we know, and meet, and love each other again."

Edith took a handkerchief from one of the pockets hidden in the folds of her cloak and noticed that she was not the only one to do so. She read out a poem of sorts that Gerald had written for the occasion.

Through the darkest day and blackest night,
Standing tall and proud
Did these fine fellows shine their light
To join us in our sacred rite.

We danced the round, and round again,
And howled up at the moon,
Making our secret plea -
Old Ones, grant our boon!

But the night was chilled,
The dancing swift and frantic,
And in the end, it did us proud,
But cost those two men dearly.

Strong of heart, stout of soul,
Full of mirth and joy, these men,
Who stood up against Hitler's insidious plan
To pay a visit to our land.

The threat is gone but still we lost:
Two fine men, gallant and true,
A sacrifice or perhaps a price,
Perhaps we shall never know.

Though tears and sorrow we will bear,
They shall not be forgotten,
For Charles and Walter will remain
Forever in our minds and hearts.

In the name of peace and love and trust,
We say farewell, as 'ere we must.

A toast was made with wine and whisky and three cheers rang out loudly, shattering the quietness of the night and startling an owl into flight nearby.

"We send you off with a drink, dear friends!" Susie shouted, tipping a little of the whisky to the ground in a tribute as the flask was passed around to her. The cheer went up again, followed by a chorus of 'jolly good fellow'.

To any outsider looking upon this group of people with their cheers and whisky, the whole affair might have appeared no more solemn an occasion than a birthday party. In truth, it was a serious matter, made more miserable by the continual drizzle of rain. Edith had had quite enough of the night, when at last, the final member of the group spoke up.

"I did not know exactly how that ritual would end, or the war itself, naturally, but I do know that each and every one of us here, tonight and on that night, would still have taken part if our destinies had been known. Walter and Charles," Rosamund stood up, taking George's hand as she rose from her little seat, "we are so very, very proud of you. We give you our humble thanks and you shall not be forgotten. Farewell."

Edith raised her arms and clapped loudly, the others joining in, one by one, to make a raucous cacophony of sound. She willed that sound to vibrate higher and higher, to be sent upon the etheric planes to whatever place or time Walter and Charles were now, hoping that somehow they would hear it and know that they were loved and remembered.

After a time, the group began to break apart and, with a final thanks to the Beloved Dead, Edith sought out Gerald and took his hand.

"It's all over."

"Yes." Gerald shook his head and gently pulled her towards him. He looked fondly into her eyes. "And yet we are only just starting out."

"What do you mean, Gerald?"

"Come, come, surely you must realise yourself that when you engineered that ritual, you were bringing together a group of people who have now become friends, and trusted ones, at that. I see many more occasions in the future when those friendships will have reason to strike up again, perhaps for high-tea or perhaps for something more."

"You do have a way with words, my dear," she held his face in one gloved hand and held her breath as he moved imperceptibly closer, "and I rather think you are right."

Gerald's face was so close to her own that their breath become one breath. "I usually am."

He moved forward, slowly. Edith closed her eyes in anticipation and then a woman's voice came between them. Several of the group were laughing over some small thing and the spell was broken. Breaking away from this dear man, who she had probably been about to kiss in way that would certainly not be described as chaste, she straightened herself up with a warm smile.

"Shall we head off now, Edith?"

She recognised her friend's voice and replied, not taking her eyes from Gerald's, "I won't be a moment, Susie."

Gerald traced the line of her jaw with his thumb, then held her face in his hands and planted a kiss on her cheek. His whiskered chin brushed against her soft skin and sent a shiver along her spine.

She pulled away, smiled, and said, "I don't know about you, but I believe it's high time to head back for a nice hot cup of cocoa before bed."

When Edith finally retired for the night, she climbed into bed with a warm blanket drawn up beneath her chin and settled down to sleep, feeling content and satisfied.

Although they had said farewell to friends this night, she felt proud to have played a part in the war effort, even if that part might never be acknowledged or appreciated.

She and her coven of witches had done all that they could.

It was, in many ways, the witches' finest hour.

Afterword by Philip Heselton

I first read Gerald Gardner's "Witchcraft Today" over 60 years ago. In it, the author made mention of a ritual that the witches of the New Forest in Hampshire performed in 1940 with the intention of stopping the invasion which was then being threatened by Hitler's forces. Gardner mentions that several of those taking part in the ritual had died as a result a few days later.

When I read that, it struck me forcibly how those events could be woven into a powerful work of fiction, and over 40 years ago I determined to write it myself.

The years passed with nothing forthcoming on my part. I remember asking a friend who was a writer of fiction whether she had ever written non-fiction. She replied, "I don't know enough to write non-fiction!" I told her I felt exactly the same but the other way around. I didn't think I knew enough to write fiction.

More years passed and I thought I would never start. Then I met Moira Hodgkinson. She had written both fiction and non-fiction, and her well-acclaimed novel "Wild Women" had just been published. She explained to me that her approach was to make the magic done by various of her characters realistic, not the sort of thing where someone waves a wand and a unicorn appears!

This was just the sort of approach I wanted in my book on the 1940 ritual. And I wanted it to be as realistic and accurate as possible, featuring the real individuals involved, what they did and why they did it.

I recounted my lack of progress on the book to Moira and she replied enthusiastically that she'd love to write it. And she has been true to her word. I handed over to her all my notes and the few passages I had already written, and Moira got down to writing immediately. I made a few comments, and she even encouraged me to write a few passages (what I called 'fragments') to slot into her text. She encouraged me just when I needed it and led me to think that my efforts were not too bad!

However, it is a work of fiction and we have both introduced scenes that probably didn't happen. But it is still a dramatic story and I hope that many, both witches and non-witches, will be inspired by it.

Philip Heselton
February 2022

Afterword by Moira Hodgkinson

When Philip first approached me with the idea of co-writing this book, I admit to feeling some amount of trepidation. After all, he is a renowned and respected author and Wiccan researcher and historian. My own books are very different: practical and experiential guides to witchcraft, along with my pagan-oriented and paranormal fantasy novels.

Philip soon put me at ease and handed over a vast amount of research, page after page of notes, dozens of books, journals, periodicals and maps that he had collected during his forty years of research. He was instrumental in organising the book into acts and scenes, which I think works very well.

While this novel is based on Philip's extensive research into events that are purported to have happened, and with people who may (or may not) have been involved, we have, of course, taken some liberties with the story, creating events, conversations and situations that suited the book as a work of fiction. It is in no way meant to be read as a factual account of the events, or indeed the people, portrayed herein, rather, it is an elaboration, a dramatic recreation, an imaginative interpretation of possible events and circumstance.

It has been a pleasure and a delight to work on the creative side of this book with Philip, whose patience, encouragement, thoughtfulness and kindness have been invaluable.

Moira Hodgkinson
Febuary 2022

About the Authors

Photo: Laura-Beth Dawson

Philip Heselton was born in 1946. He has written extensively on earth mysteries and the history of the modern witchcraft revival. He is one of the world's foremost experts on the subject and his acclaimed biographies of Gerald Gardner and Doreen Valiente were in published 2012 and 2016 respectively.

Photo: Steve Hindon Photography

Moira Hodgkinson is the author of practical books on magical practices and also writes urban fantasy pagan novels for both adults and children. She is a regular guest speaker at pagan conferences and holds open Sabbat rituals in the heart of Sherwood Forest.

www.ingramcontent.com/pod-product-compliance
Lightning Source LLC
Chambersburg PA
CBHW030036100526
44590CB00011B/231